ART
After School

A successful way to reach youth in your neighborhood

FREE After School Resource Catalog
School-Age NOTES
P.O. Box 40205
Nashville, TN 37204
1-800-410-8780
www.AfterSchoolCatalog.com

Written by
Jane Brite & Marlene Jaglinski

Illustrations by
JoAnna Poehlmann

Published by
Community Arts Consultants, LLC

Illustrations by JoAnna Poehlmann
Edited by Beth Slocum and Rhoda Sherwood
Designed by Sabine Beaupré

Printed by Malloy Lithographing, Inc.
PO Box 1124
Ann Arbor, MI 48106-1124
800-722-3231

Published with the assistance of grants from
The Milwaukee Foundation and Safe & Sound, Milwaukee, WI.

To contact the authors, address correspondence to:

Community Arts Consultants, LLC
1610 N. Prospect Avenue
Milwaukee, WI 53202

Fax: 414-963-4214
Email: jagmk@execpc.com
Phone: 414-271-1192

ISBN 0-9661021-0-X

www.artafterschool.com

Dedication

We dedicate this book to the children who participated in the Hands On after-school art program at Walker's Point Center for the Arts, and who inspired us to share the Art After School concept to benefit children everywhere.

Jane Brite & Marlene Jaglinski

 # Preface

Hands On after school art program at Walker's Point Center for the Arts is a living example of how the arts can make a difference in people's lives.

What started as an avant-garde performance and visual art center on the south side of Milwaukee, Wisconsin, evolved into a haven for children in a disadvantaged neighborhood. Children who seldom participated in making art suddenly experienced the thrill of imagining and executing their own creations. For many, it became a turning point in their lives.

As that evolution took place, the mission of the Center and its staff changed to embrace a larger vision: provide children with a window to a brighter future as well as an escape from the everyday realities of gangs and drugs.

As more and more programs were developed for children and adults, Walker's Point Center for the Arts became closely intertwined with the Walker's Point community and its residents. The learning process continued on all sides as to how art can make a difference in people's lives.

In this book, we relate our experiences in the hopes that similar programs can be established in neighborhoods throughout the country in order to reach children and help them experience the miracles that art can bring about.

The mission of Hands On has become our mission: to broaden the horizons of children whenever and wherever possible and, by so doing, to offer them a better future. We hope that this book will serve as a guide for others to develop after-school art programs that provide a creative outlet and source of inspiration for many more children.

Jane Brite & Marlene Jaglinski

Author Acknowledgements

Art After School is a book woven from experiences with Hands On, an after school art program, community organizations and leaders, boards of directors, a cadre of staff, interns, volunteers and artists at Walker's Point Center for the Arts and with neighborhood residents and businesses that recognize the positive impact the arts can have on a community.

We applaud both Beth Slocum for recognizing the promise of this project and guiding us through its evolution and JoAnna Poehlmann for her illustrations that add life and whimsy to the text. Two WPCA Board members, Phil Lerman and Jane Bekos, deserve special mention for their extraordinary support and effort as advocates of art programming for children. Special thanks to Julio Guix for years of patience and professional financial management of the Center.

We commend Ellen Checota and Barbara Kohl-Spiro for their volunteerism, talent and creativity, which laid the groundwork for the Hands On program and the *Art After School* book concept.

After-school programs cannot succeed without the generous giving of time, talent and treasure by individuals, public and private foundations and corporations. We acknowledge Jim Marks of the Milwaukee Foundation, who awarded WPCA its first grant. We are indebted to Karen Spahn of the Milwaukee Foundation, for her support of the Center's after-school art programming. She was instrumental in making this book go from concept to reality. We are most grateful to the Mary Nohl Fund of the Milwaukee Foundation and Safe & Sound for funding to create and distribute *Art After School*.

We express gratitude to the Jane Pettit, Jacobus Family, Milwaukee Board of Realtors, Kohler, and Gardner foundations for support of programming for children and the arts over the years. Corporate support from Marshall Fields & Company, Miller Brewing Company and Ronald McDonald Children's Charities of Wisconsin all made wonderful activities possible. The City of Milwaukee Arts Board, Milwaukee County funding for the arts and the Wisconsin Arts Board were all instrumental in making programs and dreams come true.

Jim Auer, art critic of *The Milwaukee Journal Sentinel*, deserves praise for his patience, advice and coverage of Center presentations.

As a bare-bones, non-profit organization, we relied upon the boundless energy of student interns from the University of Wisconsin–Milwaukee, Marquette University, Cardinal Stritch University, Wisconsin Lutheran College, Mount Mary College, Alverno College, and the Milwaukee Institute of Art & Design.

Jane is indebted to the following artist colonies for residencies to work on this project: Dorland Mountain Arts Colony, Temecula, California; Helene Wurlitzer Foundation, Taos, New Mexico; Ucross Foundation, Clearmont, Wyoming; Virginia Center for the Creative Arts, Sweet Briar, Virginia; and the Tyrone Guthrie Center, Newbliss, Ireland.

We acknowledge the patience of our families and friends as we embarked upon and completed this journey.

Jane Brite & Marlene Jaglinski

Table of Contents

Introduction

Art After School: A successful way to reach youth in your neighborhood was written as a guide, training and reference book on after-school art programming for children and teenagers. This book is based on years of experience seeing the positive impact an after-school program can have on young people, particularly in high crime areas. The primary focus of Art After School is to affirm how after-school art programming can offer a new dimension to intervention and prevention for at-risk youth, especially when presented during those hours when young people commit or are victims of crime.

Second, after-school art programs go beyond their walls to build partnerships with schools (elementary through college level), public and private agencies, and businesses to form a network of support and growth that can strengthen the entire community. Through a network of partnerships, new paradigms develop to stabilize and enrich communities.

Why include the arts in after-school programming?

Art After School focuses on using the arts and professional artists to broaden the worlds of young people, build their self-esteem, ignite creativity, develop life skills, reinforce academics and offer alternatives to inactivity. Art is easily combined with sports, homework help and other after-school activities in a variety of settings to reach more at-risk youth by providing them additional alternatives to the dangers and enticements of the streets.

Art After School is a resource to help you structure a program and keep it running. It was written as a user-friendly resource to help after-school program staff easily understand organizational concepts and finance fundamentals, including strategies and examples of how to implement them. Many studies validate the need for after-school programming and the benefits of participation in the arts for young people. Art After School can help after-school programs begin and flourish in neighborhoods anywhere. The concept is adaptable to stand-alone centers and established programs.

Art After School Authors

Jane Brite and Marlene Jaglinski have over 20 years of experience working with children and young adults in professional and volunteer positions. As director of the Walker's Point Center for the Arts in 1987, Brite initiated Hands On, a free after-school and summer art program for the primarily low-income, under-served and at-risk children and teenagers in the Walker's Point neighborhood of Milwaukee. Hands On classes were held several days per week after school and for six weeks during the summer months. Brite's 30 years of experience in the arts in Milwaukee (including over 20 years with the

Milwaukee Art Musuem) and in other cities allowed her access to professional national and local artists who would work with students at Walker's Point Center for the Arts. Hands On grew to serve as many as 1,500 children and young adults annually.

Marlene Jaglinski was administrator at Walker's Point Center for the Arts for several years. She brought corporate management skills from the Continental Can Company and VISTA experience as a volunteer in community economic and educational development. At the Center she prepared budgets, grant proposals, publicity and schedules. She supervised staffing and other administrative functions. She has successfully written grants for a variety of civic and art groups, directed to local, state and national government units as well as corporate and individual donors. Marlene was a leader with Girl Scout and Boy Scout troops and has worked with church youth programs. Through experience with business and civic organizations, she brings an understanding of their needs and goals and shows how to blend them into partnerships for young people.

The authors forged partnerships with area colleges and universities to recruit student interns to work with children and teenagers to give the children an opportunity to learn from young adults.

Although the majority of the children served were ages 6 through 12, Brite and Jaglinski administered projects that targeted 12- through 18- year-olds, many of whom were gang members. These teenagers participated in mural painting, photography, public art and performance projects. A number of the teenagers chose to stay in school and some have gone on to jobs in art-related fields after their art experiences. Brite and Jaglinski serve on the boards of and consult for various arts organizations.

Why add an art component to after-school programming?

Art is that part of a school curriculum often considered a frill and the first to go when there is a dollar crunch. But it is a godsend for children who have limited opportunity for expression and inquiry. This concept works for all young people but offers startling results for those considered at risk. By participating in the arts in a non-judgmental, positive environment, young people can open, grow, comprehend and accept the world. The arts unlock creativity in children, enabling them to adjust to challenges and opportunities in their lives.

Art provides young people opportunities that:
    Teach problem-solving skills and techniques
    Reinforce academics
    Stir imaginations and the creative spirit
    Provide a way to release feelings in a positive way
    Celebrate individuality
    Make them aware of art and their surroundings
    Develop awareness and understanding of art in cultural heritage

Artists offer a fresh perspective.

We advocate using artists to work with children in after-school programs. Artists are capable of small wonders. They are free-thinking and experimental, creating environments that are stimulating and entertaining. Risk is often their by-word when it involves looking at things from different perspectives. Painting a banana blue or a cow purple gives a new perspective on everyday objects that is whimsical and refreshing. The opportunity for artists to work with children offers unique multi-cultural as well as cross-generational experiences.

Children Ages 10 Through 16

Many after-school programs focus on children 6 to 10 years old. Targeting children over ten and through the teenage years presents special considerations. *Art After School* details several successful projects with teenagers who participated in the Hands On, after-school art program. One project allowed gang members to do a show of graffiti on the gallery walls. The show did not glamorize gangs or graffiti. It gave participants an opportunity to express in a controlled environment what gangs do and why they do it. It gave the public an opportunity to talk with these young people to see that behind the tough façade are real life-and-death fears and a need to belong. While two local police officers were walking their beat, they came into the Center to see what the teens were doing. A long dialogue occurred between the teens and the police officers. In the end both "sides" had a better understanding of each other's goals and concerns. The police officers bought t-shirts the teens had painted.

Offer Young People Art as an Alternative

Art activities do not need to be confined within walls, nor is art found only in museums. A familiar neighborhood site offering art is not intimidating but welcoming. Young people enjoy doing public art such as murals on a neighborhood building. They learn how to use the arts in small ways to enhance their neighborhoods. Successful collaboration with business and local governments gives young people visibility and opportunities to learn skills and earn money. The arts can be a bridge to other activities. Sports and art can be combined as students design team t-shirts or enhance a basketball court or a gym.

Safe & Sound is a community-based, anti-crime initiative in Milwaukee, Wisconsin, designed to attack the problem of youth crime through positive alternatives for youth, neighborhood organizing and tough law enforcement. Safe & Sound Safe Place sites are located in a variety of settings, including public and private schools, churches and youth centers. They offer art programming to provide young people with additional options for positive activities during those hours when they are statistically more susceptible to committing crimes or being victims of crime.

Young people need to talk about critical issues that affect them every day, including gangs, crime and pregnancy. Young people can dig deeper into their souls for expression through role playing, writing about their fears and concerns, acting them out through performances, or creating art pieces to express feelings on difficult topics.

A Success Story

Six months after WPCA opened, a neighborhood teenager named Oscar Rodriguez offered to be a volunteer. The art and artists he saw working at the Center intrigued him. He kept the gallery open on weekends. He learned to hang exhibits and organize receptions, planning everything from buying refreshments to clean-up. He dealt with some difficult demands by artists and helped with technical needs such as lighting and sound requirements. He even helped build stages for performances.

Oscar worked with many famous artists, including performance artist Karen Finley. He was her right-hand man in the technical aspects of her performance.

Through these experiences, Oscar's talent and enthusiasm for the arts blossomed and Center staff helped him attain a scholarship to the Pratt Institute in New York. When Karen Finley came to Pratt to do a performance, Oscar contacted her. She remembered him and asked him to work with her again.

Oscar graduated from the Milwaukee Institute of Art & Design with a major in design and a minor in photography. He has a promising career in the marketing department of a manufacturing firm.

Similar opportunities for young people have arisen at the Center. Through trial and error, limited only by the boundaries of our collective imagination, we worked as a unit. There was no right or wrong, good or bad idea. Time and money were our only constraints. We tried innovative programs and often pushed the limits.

It is said that creative people are committed to risk. Just keeping the door open was often very difficult, but we kept the spirit alive in all our endeavors. We were always willing to push beyond the routine.

Academic Achievement

Studies show there are many ways to learn. Noted education authority Howard Gardner, in his book *Multiple Intelligences*, reports findings on the various ways humans learn. He proposes that we should all be given alternative ways to learn. Some people learn and understand concepts best by hearing them, some learn best through reading and others learn by doing. Often the most effective learning occurs when material is presented in two or more formats. Using the arts to reinforce or introduce academic material is a well-proven method of facilitating education. We worked with a Milwaukee kindergarten-through-fifth grade school to host an artist for a two-week residency art project to reinforce the environmental theme being emphasized in the class course work.

A paper maker worked with the students to teach them how to produce paper pulp from cotton rags, pound pulp into various paper forms and connect those forms into a permanent mural for their media center. The artist met with the teachers before the project began to find out what the children would be learning in their classrooms and then used her time with them to talk about environmental issues while they were working on the handmade paper mural. As a result of the in-class learning and hands-on activities, the children learned about environmental issues and actively participated in recycling while making art. Hanging in their school is a daily reminder of what the students learned about adaptive re-use of materials.

Recreational Programs

Arts and crafts are effective components of a recreational program. These activities can be active or quiet, individual or group, indoors or outdoors. Found objects, cans and boxes can be used to make a percussion band. Students can do individual projects or group projects that use group dynamics to plan and reach the desired goal. They can paint flowerpots indoors on a rainy day and then take them outdoors to create an urban garden.

Young people should be encouraged to suggest the type of projects they would like to do. They need to feel ownership by being involved in and responsible for participation in all aspects of a project. Parents should always be encouraged to attend art-making sessions and make art alongside the children. It is our experience that parents and older siblings who initially shy away from participating in art projects usually become engrossed in making art and feel comfortable returning to participate.

Personal and Interpersonal Development

Making art involves planning ahead and making choices. It also encourages starting over and finding alternative ways to achieve the desired result. Art encourages freedom of thought. A successful program doesn't censure the art created. The teacher or artist is a guide, not a master. Young people are encouraged to do individual projects that reflect their personal tastes and direction. Group activities encourage all aspects of project development from idea to completion.

Art is a powerful way to diffuse violence and frustration. It helps one deal with the pain experienced in parts of life one may not understand and allows young people to express frustration and anger through their art rather than though violence.

The arts provide a window into cross-cultural understanding. Making art offers time for personal pleasure and enjoyment.

Community Partnerships and Collaborations

Art After School gives details on how to develop partnerships and collaborations with community groups and businesses. However, don't limit yourself to organizations that are associated with the arts. Think about the needs of the young people participating and about community needs. For example, include law enforcement officers on your list of volunteers. When police officers and young people work together planning, implementing and completing art projects, they get to know each other as individuals, not just members of the "other side."

How To Establish an Art After School Program in Your Community

The mission and goals of a program can vary widely and will change over time to reflect the needs of your neighborhood. Determine a mission statement for your program. Establish a strategic plan to carry out your organizational vision through a set of achievable goals. Always consider your program within the context of the broader community. Programming will be most effective if it reflects and correlates with the needs and vision of the neighborhood.

An after-school art program model is a simple concept adaptable to many settings. It does not have to be located in an art center. It can operate in a stand-alone location or be integrated into on-going after-school or summer programs. The concept can impact all children by nurturing their talents, building their self-esteem and encouraging them to make positive choices, while giving them a safe place to just be kids (but it is especially effective for those children considered at risk). The program can be effective with either meager or abundant budgets. This book is based upon real-life experiences. It gives background on the Hands On, after-school art program concept to help you have a positive influence on the children in your community through the arts.

Art After School fills a need

Too many children are in crisis. Impoverished children disconnected from a nurturing home often learn life from the streets. Drugs, gangs and violence are pervasive forces that steal the innocence of childhood from our children. Children need to be children. They need safe places to dream, create, experiment, build self-esteem and do things that feed the soul. Schools are asked not only to teach, but also to act as surrogate parents by carrying out tasks that were formerly part of a family's domain.

For a few hours a week, at an after-school art program, children can escape difficult circumstances to participate in exciting opportunities for expression, opportunities that also reinforce academic subjects.

This neighborhood art center model is endorsed by educators who have seen what a tremendous impact involvement in the arts can have on a child's life. Not every child is a success story. However, the arts can reach every child in a positive way.

"We began classes when school cutbacks had all but abolished art programs and after-school activities. The Center filled this gap. We had a small space and limited resources, but we were full of ideas and we had a lot of friends. We used and abused them all. We were forced to be innovative. We were forced to be creative. We became adept moochers and creative recyclers. As a result, the children interacted with a number of local artist friends and worked in a wide range of media.

"We constructed Halloween masks and made Christmas ornaments. We decorated tennis shoes donated by Target. We painted t-shirts—which aided the creative spirit and provided a fun piece of clothing the children could wear to school. We drew on walls and sidewalks and made outdoor spaces. We had art shows that presented our work to the community. We drew ourselves and in the process revealed ourselves. We learned from each other. But best of all, we became friends."

Ellen Checota
Artist/Teacher

The arts—that part of the school curriculum often considered a frill and the first to go when there is a dollar crunch—can be a godsend for children who have limited opportunity for expression and inquiry. Art After School is not just for the good kids; this concept works with startling results for the fringe child, the one who does not get involved, who hates school, the at-risk child. Through participation in the arts in a positive environment young people blossom, grow, comprehend and accept the world. They learn to appreciate the creativity that is distinctly their own. The goal of an after-school art program is to unlock the creativity in children, giving them new ways to learn and teaching them skills needed to interact and communicate with people. These skills are vital to their ability to function in the world and to adjust to challenges and opportunities in life. Art education encourages initiative, inventiveness and the ability to adapt to constantly changing situations. Art gives us new eyes and ears to make us all more aware of and in touch with each other and our surroundings.

Participation in the arts provides children opportunities that:
- Stir imaginations and the creative spirit
- Offer a way to release feelings in a positive way
- Celebrate individuality
- Focus on the value of creative expression
- Encourage a sense of pleasure in their own creativity
- Build confidence and pride in their creations and themselves
- Foster the unique nature of self expression
- Show the relationship between art and the environment
- Reinforce academic principles through the arts
- Develop awareness and understanding of art in cultural heritage
- Heighten problem-solving skills and techniques
- Introduce a variety of community professionals and artists

Art fosters creativity by encouraging each child to trust their instincts and vision. They aren't judged—just given positive reinforcement so they experience the freedom of the creative process. This encourages children to:
- Enjoy the process and outcome of art experiences
- Think logically and abstractly
- Learn artistic principles
- Communicate ideas, thoughts, feelings and needs in various ways
- Learn strategies to cope with the challenges of daily life
- Set short-and long-term goals
- Become aware of career opportunities
- Improvise

Art After School can be unique in providing direct creative experiences in the visual, literary and performing arts in a warm and spontaneous environment.

Christopher

One day when the children were off from school, 10-year-old Christopher, who lived next door to the Center, stopped by to visit several times. Because of the dangers in the neighborhood, his mother restricted him to either their home or the Center. Christopher was at an age targeted by gangs to get new recruits. At the Center, he often volunteered to make photocopies or stuff envelopes for mailings. He began attending the after-school art classes when he was six years old and after four years was familiar with Center operations and friends with all the staff.

On one particular day, Chris came to the Center several times to borrow a different item: first a bottle of glue, then paper clips, then a paintbrush. On his fourth trip, he brought a magnificent model made on a piece of cardboard about the size of a cardtable top. He had taped and glued odd pieces of cardboard together to make a soccer field, day-care center, basketball court, hotel and golf course for a dream city. Everything was created from toothpicks, scraps of paper, bottle caps and other found objects!

When Chris first attended the after-school art classes, he had not displayed any particular artistic tendencies. However, his dream city is a confirmation that encouragement and affirmation release not only the ability to be creative but the joy that comes from creating something for personal pleasure and to share with others.

The Arts Open Windows

Many children such as seven year-old Tony were tentative about their first art experiences. Children like Tony would use only black or dark colors during their first few sessions at the Center. Slowly they begin to feel comfortable using brighter materials. After attending classes for a few weeks, Tony proudly displayed his latest brightly colored work. Over time his face also brightened as he smiled more.

Robert Koeper, Vieau Elementary School principal, frequently brought his seventh grade students to participate in daytime or after-school special events. When asked why he included the seventh grade students more often than the other grades, he commented that *after seventh grade the students are lost to the system.* They become more interested in the temptations of the street than they are in school. He said that students need to enjoy being in school and find it worth their time, or they drop out. *He welcomed every chance to reach seventh graders because this was his last chance to influence them.* He hoped these positive experiences would show them that education can be exciting and a way to open doors for them in the future.

11

After-school art programs offer students a safe haven from negative influences. Students considered at risk or misfits often give up on school and drop out to spend their time on the streets. However, after positive experiences in the arts, they blossom. They take pride in their accomplishments and themselves, making it easier for them to choose to stay in school and take positive rather then negative paths.

When ten-year-old Ulanda first attended after-school art classes, she could not read, nor could she start or finish a project without extensive help. Although quiet, withdrawn and unsure of herself for many reasons (including the fact that she could not read), Ulanda kept coming to class. The first project she worked on was coloring sand to make a layered design in a clear glass bottle. She had great difficulty with this project. After several months she asked the teacher to make sand bottles again. This time Ulanda not only made her sand bottle without help, she taught the other children how to make them!

An after-school art program can have an impact whether finances are meager or abundant, surroundings are opulent or rough, or the setting is rural or urban. The most important aspect is to develop a caring relationship with a child while providing the tools for expression in a carefree environment.

Build Community Through Art

Art After School builds community by encouraging interaction among educators, artists, social service groups, businesses and neighbors. The arts celebrate every child's individuality as well as the cultural diversity and richness of a neighborhood. Few things are as pleasing to a community as seeing their children happily walking down the street carrying their latest artistic creations.

Educators, community groups, churches, artist groups and employers as well as museums, art centers, colleges and universities can use this concept to reach out to children in a variety of settings. The possibilities are endless and the rewards great—not only for the children but for the entire community because through these collaborations, formal and informal networking occurs that brings together people and groups that would otherwise not interact.

Principal Koeper saw what a difference the after-school art program had on his students, especially at-risk children. After seeing the positive reactions of children and artists at the Center, he hired local artists as teacher aides. At-risk children worked with the artists who, through simple art projects, helped the children reinforce academics.

12

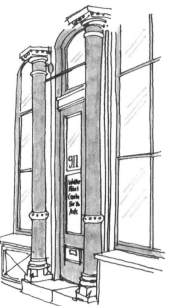

chapter

2

Selecting a Site

An after-school art program can begin on folding tables in almost any well-lit room. An art center would be an ideal location because children have a variety of experiences as exhibits change. However, an after-school arts program does not need to be located in an art center or even a stand-alone facility. It can successfully share space in a variety of venues since classes are held after school, during the day in summer, or on weekends. Shared space can reduce program costs.

The basic requirements for an after-school art program are simple: a room about 25' x 30' x 60', a source of water, bathroom facilities, storage units, good lighting and electrical outlets and a place to prepare light snacks.

Visibility and accessibility for pedestrians and vehicles are also key factors. Windows or outside space to display artwork help attract children and visitors to see what your program is all about.

> *"It was a good idea to have classes on busy National Avenue. Everybody walking by stops to look at the kids' art or pictures on display in the front windows. People look at photographs of the kids or art by their kids, cousins or neighbors. I like when my Mom sees what we do in class."*
>
> *Maria*
> *Hands On, Art After School student*

When evaluating potential sites consult this checklist:
- Is the site within walking distance of area schools?
- Can the children cross streets safely to get to the site?
- Is the site safe and does it meet local building codes?
- Is the lighting (natural and artificial) adequate?
- Is there proper ventilation?
- Are stairs, doors and walkways well lit and in good repair?
- Are there taverns, drug houses or other potentially dangerous businesses nearby?

Interior features to consider :
- An area for coats and backpacks
- A restroom near the work space
- A slop sink for cleaning brushes, etc.
- Another sink for hand washing and food preparation
- Flooring that can be easily swept and washed
- Storage area for supplies and works in progress
- A locked storage area for valuable items: cameras, film, compact disc/tape players, VCR or TV set, microphones, etc.
- Wall and floor space to display artwork
- An outdoor area for classes and other activities

Nice to have:
- Gallery space away from the work area to display art
- Outdoor garden to incorporate science and art themes
- Bookshelves for a lending library
- Refrigerator
- Microwave oven/gas or electric stove

Finding a Great Location

Have a budget in mind for rent, repairs, site preparation, utilities and insurance before you start looking for a location. Target the part of town in which you wish to locate and then look through newspaper ads for rental properties. Also talk to real estate agents and local business people for word-of-mouth recommendations on available storefronts and other properties.

Enlist one or two members of your Board of Directors and someone knowledgeable about building repairs and codes to help evaluate available sites. Go as a group to look at properties. Evaluate each one against your criteria and budget considerations.

Drive and walk around the neighborhood at different times during the day, after school, evenings and weekends to see what kind of activity goes on in the area. Find out how many children live in the immediate vicinity and within two to three blocks of a site. Look at how many busy streets the children must cross and what the traffic is like during the times they would be coming to and going from the center.

You also need to consider who the neighbors are. Will the kids cause annoyance when they are noisy? Or do the neighbors offer potential dangers to the children? Do not locate near drug houses, taverns and other places where the clientele is not appropriate for children.

The potential cost of bringing a building up to usable standards often prevented us from choosing it. We found a wonderful old warehouse but the renovation would have been too expensive. It was four blocks from a residential area and the children would have to cross several busy streets to get there, so we did not take it.

When you find a property that meets your criteria, try negotiating with the owner. If you don't feel comfortable doing this, ask a board member to negotiate for you. Negotiate not only rent but also repairs to be done before you move in, as well as ongoing maintenance such as snow shoveling and plumbing repairs, etc. Discuss the length of a lease. A lease for three-to-five years instead of one year shows commitment and allows the building owner to amortize repair costs over a period of time.

Emphasize to the landlord that an after-school program in the building benefits the immediate neighborhood as well as adding to his or her image as a person concerned about the area. Suggest that the owner give back to the community by offering a break on the rent, not charging for repair and remodeling costs, or guaranteeing a low rent and a long-term lease with options for renewal. Be concerned and frank about insurance coverage.

Having a grocery and hardware store nearby is very handy. Restaurants nearby are a convenience when entertaining potential funders or media representatives who visit the program. Visiting artists and others who work long hours to prepare for classes or exhibits appreciate a nearby eatery. Also, patronizing local businesses helps you get to know your neighbors. They in turn will support you even if you bring only a small amount of business to them through your activities. You can partner with a barber, a small grocery store on the next block, an auto body shop, or even a tire store for the benefit of the whole neighborhood. Work with stores to display fliers and artwork and encourage neighborhood residents to volunteer. The business owners recognize the importance of having area children occupied in positive activities.

Storefronts

Storefronts make great after-school art centers. They are user-friendly and accessible. They have large windows for natural light and a highly visible place to display finished art or works in progress. Revitalizing an abandoned five-and-dime or small department store can have a dramatic effect on a block. Increased traffic by parents and others to see what the children are doing in the after-school program encourages traffic to other stores in the area.

Art galleries, art centers, artists and students often move into rundown neighborhoods because of low rents, interesting architecture and convenience. These activities can help revitalize a neighborhood.

"Showing our art work and pictures of the kids in the front windows was great for the kids and the neighbors to see what we do. Being located on a main street gives the program visibility and encourages people walking by to stop and look or come into the Center."

Chris
Hands On, Art After School student

A long-term lease with renewal options will help you maintain a reasonable rent even if property values begin to rise in the area. Do not try to gentrify an area. Respect area residents and business owners. Become a helpful, vital part of the community.

Suggestions for Shared Venues

An after-school art program can be set up as a satellite center in lofts above businesses, in schools or in church basements. Here are some suggested liaisons for space.

Libraries

I hate lies
I hate pigs
I hate brothers
I hate movies
But what I like
is Poetry!
Adriana
Walker's Point Young Poets
Book 1989

Disadvantaged children often lack access to books and magazines. Housing an after-school art program in a neighborhood library encourages children to visit the library and learn to use its facilities while participating in after-school art experiences. The Milwaukee Art Museum and other organizations throughout the country have partnered with neighborhood libraries to share space for art programming. This is a good way to take art to the neighborhoods and to reach children and adults who do not usually take part in museum activities.

A college art education department could invite its students to collaborate with neighborhood libraries to incorporate after-school art experiences into their programming. This offers college students a training opportunity to work with disadvantaged children as well as diverse ethnic populations.

Surrounding children with books is a tremendous resource for ideas because it intermingles academics and art. Art by the children can be displayed on library walls and bookcases or in entrance areas. To create some library collaborative programming:

- Invite authors and book illustrators to teach the children to write poetry or stories as well as to illustrate their writing.
- Have the children write stories about their art.
- Encourage them to write about art they find in library books.
- Encourage children to perform skits or read works they have written for parents and the public.

Public and Private Schools

Include art programming along with other after-school activities, for instance sports and clubs such as Girl Scouts or Boy Scouts. Art activities can be integrated with other activities to satisfy badge and advancement requirements for Scouting, 4-H or other youth programs. Activities can be designed to reinforce academics for children who need academic support.

Add an art component to other ongoing programs even when not located on the same site. We collaborated with two neighborhood youth centers that sponsored after-school, evening and weekend sports programs. However, not all the young people were into sports or wanted to do sports all the time. The youth centers transported a van-load of students to the Center twice a week for art classes. They paid a fee to cover supplies and teacher/artist time. Their staff stayed to help with classes and take the students back to their youth center. This was an easy and workable arrangement.

Churches

Many churches have basements or other space available during after school hours. These sites would satisfy the physical requirements for an after-school art program and provide the church an opportunity to serve community needs beyond its own congregation. The church might welcome a small stipend to help cover their building costs, and the congregation would enjoy a changing display of artwork by the children.

Meal Programs and Senior Centers

These services are located in accessible venues that meet local building codes and have tables and chairs. Art classes can be conducted at a meal program site between lunch and dinner times or after the dinner serving. A few tables can be designated for class use and separated from food preparation and serving areas.

At these public sites the children have an audience for their paintings, sculpture or photography. Mingling children, teachers and senior citizens encourages multi-generation projects and collaborations.

Manufacturing Plants

As manufacturing plants move from inner city locations to suburban areas, empty buildings in the city may offer options for housing an after-school art program. An area of the plant that was a lunchroom or office space can be converted into an art education studio.

Seasonal and Migrant Worker Locations

Art After School is most effective when children participate in the program over a period of time. However, the children of seasonal or migrant workers can also benefit from even a few sessions. These children rarely have formal exposure to the arts. They often face language barriers and are frequently pulled from one school experience to another as their families move. It is important that artists and teachers be sensitive to the social, cultural and economic conditions of the children.

Fluency in the native language of the children is critical. A sensitive, caring instructor can use the arts to help these children deal with uncertainties and hardships while celebrating the good aspects of their lives. They can be encouraged to express their feelings and hopes through their art.

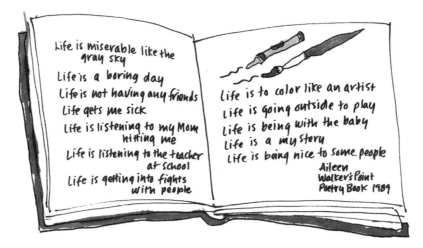

Life is miserable like the gray sky
Life is a boring day
Life is not having any friends
Life gets me sick
Life is listening to my Mom hitting me
Life is listening to the teacher at school
Life is getting into fights with people

Life is to color like an artist
Life is going outside to play
Life is being with the baby
Life is a mystery
Life is being nice to some people
Aileen
Walker's Point
Poetry Book 1989

Classes can be held on picnic tables in a park, under a tent near the fields where the parents are working or in an unused barn or outbuilding. The important factor is the caring relationship between adult and child that occurs while the program provides opportunities for self-expression.

Supplies can be simple: paper, crayons or found objects. The paper can be drawn on, written on or folded to make origami shapes or airplanes. Children should be encouraged to use inexpensive, easily available materials so they can learn to make art out of everyday items. For example, found objects can be used to make incredible sculpture pieces. Read poetry or stories to the children and then ask them to change the ending or create another chapter to encourage oral storytelling that they can do when books in their native language are not available.

Other Possible Partnerships and Venues

- Recreation departments
- Head Start/daycare/after-school programs
- Church outreach programs
- College/university art and/or education departments
- Empty auto dealer showrooms or movie theaters
- Boys and girls clubs
- YMCA/YWCA/Future Farmer organizations
- Girl Scout/Boy Scout troops
- Community centers
- Museums/art centers
- Social service agencies

Making art is an interactive concept. Encourage children to participate in all activities, from ideas to clean up. Pay more attention to the children than to the color of the walls. Children come to love and respect their art center when they share in the responsibility of caring for it. They will take pride in themselves and the place that fosters encouragement and respect, one that allows them just to be kids. **An Art After School program can work almost anywhere. Be creative.**

chapter

3

Financial Plan and Budgets

To establish a financial plan for your organization, consult with a certified public accountant and an attorney familiar with the legal and tax issues associated with setting up a non-profit versus a for-profit organization. These people will advise you on the accounting and legal practices to follow as well as taxes, employment taxes, wage laws and other reporting requirements that you must abide by on local, state and federal levels. They will also advise you on filing appropriate forms for employees, independent contractors and others paid by your program.

Work with an accountant to learn standard accounting procedures and how to account for income, expenses and in-kind donations. Keep accurate, up-to-date records and have your finances audited annually or every other year.

First Things First—Your Tax Status

Unless your program is under the umbrella of an Internal Revenue tax exempt institution, you should apply for tax exempt status as a "not for profit" organization with the Internal Revenue Service as soon as possible. Many funding bodies will give money only to non-profit organizations as determined by the United States Internal Revenue Service. Funding agencies require you to submit a copy of the IRS determination letter with proposal requests and applications. Contact the IRS for guidelines and application forms. Discuss the application with a tax attorney and certified public accountant before submitting it to the Internal Revenue Service to avoid processing delays.

Your organization may be exempt from state sales tax. Contact your state department of revenue for guidelines and forms to determine if your organization qualifies for exempt tax status.

In the category for wages, include all aspects of the cost of an employee in your budget, such as state and federal tax liabilities, social security, Medicare, and state unemployment tax liabilities, as well as benefit costs for insurance, 401K programs, etc.

Your organization should have your financial records audited—annually or at least every other year to demonstrate your financial integrity.

Basically you will be working with two types of budgets: **Program** and **Project** budgets.

The **Program Budget** takes into consideration all the factors necessary to carry on your after-school program: rent, utilities, supplies, wages, insurance, etc.

Project Budgets focus on the expenses and income directly attributable to a particular project. For example, hiring an artist to work with six children to create a sculpture piece is an individual project that is just one part of your overall program of activities.

Program Budget

Variables such as class size and frequency of meeting, the number of paid and volunteer staff, and rented versus a rent-free site all influence your program budget. Salaries, rent, art and office supplies and equipment, insurance, electricity, heat and air conditioning costs, telephone, promotional materials and snacks all represent major budget components.

We did not charge children to attend after-school classes because of the economic level of the neighborhood population. We did not want to turn away any child who could not pay. Nor did we want to administer a sliding scale or other financial-need formula. We preferred to have the children "give back" by having them help with class set-up and clean-up or weeding and watering the garden. We occasionally asked the children to make an extra piece of art to use for fundraising, thank you gifts to donors, sales at functions or displays at the Center.

> *"I spent a lot of my free time at the Center because I liked to be around the people. I volunteered to make copies on the copier or stuff envelopes for mailings. It was interesting to hear everyone always talking about raising money. When I think back, it is amazing that you did so much at the Center, especially for Hands On, with so little money."*
>
> *Chris Vega*
> *Hands On, Art After School Participant and Neighbor*

Prepare a realistic budget for your first year of operation. After deducting start-up costs (one-time expenses necessary to initiate a program) and including a component for growth, make realistic budget predictions for two years beyond your first year. A three-year budget gives you an economic and strategic plan for programming and funding. You may want to add 10 percent to years two and three to account for increased costs.

Be flexible. Your budget may have extreme annual fluctuations depending upon the amount of financial support from corporations and individual donors, collaborations, volunteers and interns and the number of children participating.

For example, you may receive $15,000 to fund a specific project for one year. You must find a way to cover the overhead costs covered by that project grant. Your budget may show great fluctuations in income and expenses from year to year because funding is often for particular projects that last for short periods of time. Be prepared to explain these budget fluctuations as an addendum to your financial statements.

Start-up Costs

You need to budget for the following to initiate an after-school arts program:
- Staff time to plan, organize and obtain program funding
- Rent deposits
- Office supplies and signs
- Program fliers, brochures and correspondence to promote program
- Internal Revenue Service non-profit and state tax-exempt filing fees
- Site preparation, conformance to codes, permits and licenses
- Cleaning, painting and lighting
- Tables, chairs, desk, computer, printer and copier
- Telephone
- Materials to create project samples
- Insurance

Cash Versus In-kind Expenses

Talk with an accountant about current tax rulings on how to list donated goods or services as "In-kind" on budgets and financial statements. Most non-profit organizations compute the hourly wage you would have to pay for donated clerical, maintenance or professional services. Multiply the estimated wage rate times the number of hours donated by each volunteer. You will find your volunteers to be an absolute treasure when you estimate their dollar worth.

To determine the value of goods, ask the donor or use actual cost. For example, if a store donates 10 gallons of paint valued at $10 per gallon, you can account for the paint as a $100 In-kind donation. In-kind income is usually applicable toward the cash match often required by funding agencies.

Be honest and accurate when determining all budget items. Be realistic and watchful throughout the process to assure that spending reflects projections. If there are deviations of more than 10 percent in any area, flag this on reports submitted. Show how you adjusted for unexpected overages and shortfalls. It is important to adhere to budgets as much as possible.

What follows is a sample after-school art program budget. In this example, classes are held 45 weeks per year, with two sessions per day, four days per week during the summer, and with five after-school sessions during the school year. The education coordinator supervised outreach activities and arranged special projects throughout the year, reaching 1,000 to 1,500 children at the Center and through outreach activities annually.

Hands On Program Budget*

Education coordinator (20-25 hours per week)

Salary and benefits	$18,000
Professional artists, $20-$25 per two-hour session	7,800
Aide to walk children to Center and assist children with projects	600
Nutritious snacks: fresh fruit, peanut butter sandwiches, fruit juice, milk, cheese, vegetables	1,000
Class supplies: markers, paint, paper, brushes, clay, crayons, glitter, beads, rulers, pencils, scissors, chalk, picture frames, t-shirts, hats, socks, feathers, jewelry supplies, fabric, yarn, cameras, film, wood, wire, nails, tools, paper cutter, hole puncher	3,500
Publicity and fliers to schools, homes, agencies	400
Rent and utilities: prorated 1/3 of total Center budget to art education	2,400
Insurance	600
Miscellaneous	500
Total program costs:	$ 34,000

*This budget is for a class of about 25 children

Project Budgets

Project Budgets have many of the same variables as the Program Budget; however, you allocate them differently and allow for special costs and possible income sources associated with the particular project.

This is important: Many funding agencies will fund specific projects but not requests for operating expenses such as rent, light, heat and staff time. However, you cannot conduct even a small project without these necessities. Therefore, pro-rate certain program operating costs such as staff salaries, utilities and rent necessary to implement the project and include them in the project budget.

Auto-Art Project Budget

Expenses:	Cash	In-kind
Director and education coordinator salaries	$1,000	$1,000
Artist	1,000	
Two design students	800	
Use of Center space		600
Marketing and recruitment of participants	200	
Paint and materials	500	
Total expenses:	$3,500	$1,600
Income:		
Contributions from businesses	590	
Foundation funds	500	
Board fundraising activities	500	
City Arts Board grant funds requested	2,410	
In-kind contributions		$1,600
Total income:	$3,500	

The in-kind contribution of $1,600 is a cash match by the Center's Board of Directors. They raised money through appeals and other fundraising activities to cover these operating expenses. The salaries of personnel involved as well as Center rent were pro-rated for the time of the project and then included in the project budget.

chapter 4

Program Staffing

A variety of factors will influence your staffing needs: the program budget, the number of children participating, school collaborations, and the number of after-school art sessions offered each week as well as the intensity and scope of program offerings.

The basic criteria for evaluating prospective staff members or volunteers are their willingness and ability to interact with each child as an individual while encouraging creativity and expression through art.

An after-school art program is not the end, but the journey.

Encourage openness through patience. Arrange for artists to teach classes as often as possible. Artists can be great teachers because they often approach a situation with fresh perspectives. Children need time with less structure, less rote and fewer demands. They need guidance and assurance for creativity to bloom. They need encouragement to color outside the lines.

The focus of an after-school art program is to have a positive impact on children whose circumstances do not afford them the opportunity for expression, for building self-esteem and for the adventure that regular exposure to and immersion in the arts can provide. Encouraging children to think freely and creatively enhances identity and aids academic and everyday life.

> *"The children remind me of little wild flowers struggling to grow in the cracks of a sidewalk. By adding a little water and light, they blossom. Art, for them, is a proclamation. A joyous way for them to shout, here I am!"*
>
> *Katie Corsmeier*
> *Hands On Teacher*

Children need mentors to encourage them to look at things in new ways, to see options and opportunities. Children from homes where English is a second language are extremely hesitant to act freely in new situations. They often feel "different" or "lacking" among peers at school. Abused children and children surrounded by those who abuse alcohol and drugs are also reticent about expressing themselves. These children are reluctant to risk saying or doing the "wrong" thing, fearful that they will draw attention to themselves and their private lives.

Often these children are at first quiet and hesitant. They use only dark colors in their work. Eventually they open up when they feel safe to do so. Those children who are starved for attention frequently interrupt, follow the teacher around or are mischievous. However, once a child feels comfortable, the pendulum swings from reclusive and dependent to confident and independent. It is a marvelous thing to see.

Personnel Considerations

1. All staff—paid and volunteer—should complete a standard employment application. General employment applications are available at most office supply stores. In this way you will have basic information about each person as well as a listing of their educational backgrounds, work histories and references.

2. It is critical that references be verified and criminal background checks be done on applicants for paid, volunteer or intern positions.

3. Job descriptions that define the specific duties should be prepared for each job. The job description should include who the person reports to and duties to be performed.

4. New employees or volunteers should receive a general orientation about the organization's history, current operations and future goals. They should have adequate training time with an experienced person. A manual with general information about your organization, mission, history, resources and staff should be available to all employees and volunteers.

When planning staffing needs, ask yourself: What duties are needed? What background or qualifications are needed to accomplish these tasks? Should these duties be performed by a paid employee, a volunteer or a college intern? Then draw up an organizational chart.

Here is a sample organizational chart:

Board of Directors
- fund raising
- legal
- accounting

Director
- fund raising
- general operations
- staffing/employment issues
- community outreach
- budgets/finances
- volunteer/intern management

Education Coordinator	Administrator	Maintenance
recruits children	writes grants	performs regular
hires teachers/artists	administers grants	cleaning
develops class schedule	handles correspondence	does minor repairs
determines projects	handles publicity	paints as needed
procures supplies	recruits interns	maintains walks
collaborates with schools	trains interns	
supervises college interns	runs office	
helps publicize program	helps with fund raising	
coordinates artist residencies	coordinates volunteers	
helps with fund raising		

Be creative, yet pragmatic. Program staff must be able to work together and brainstorm. Projects and programs can grow from a little idea bounced around among staff and interns at a weekly staff meeting. Non-profit organizations must be flexible. Every staff member must be prepared to wear a variety of hats.

Board of Directors

Keeping the program fiscally sound is their prime responsibility. Unless your program is under the umbrella of another organization, you should have a Board of Directors. It can consist of concerned business, professional and neighborhood people, including parents, teachers, school administrators and artists. They help with fund raising, accounting, legal and other issues by networking through business contacts and community, school and professional organizations.

The Board of Directors is responsible for hiring the Director. Job duties determine other position titles. It is important that the Board and Director have a good working relationship.

Members of a Board of Directors should get to know each other and be able to work together. They should all be familiar with the organization's goals, mission and strategies for implementing programs and development. They should be familiar with the organization's history and long-term plan.

An ideal board would include a lawyer, accountant, elementary school principal, teacher, artist, community leader, marketing or public relations person, someone with ties to a foundation to find funding opportunities, a development person to focus on fund raising as well as members-at-large willing to be worker bees.

The Board should reflect the community and the children served. Include board members of both genders who represent area cultural and ethnic groups. A diverse board will help you achieve your goals and impress funding agencies.

> *"The opportunity for children to interact with real artists, particularly children at risk, is what drew me to Walker's Point Center for the Arts. The added bonus was that the artists were always first rate and enjoyed their experiences with the kids as well as the kids' enjoying the opportunity to meet and work with the artists. The whole concept was a memorable and extraordinary experience for all involved."*
>
> *Michael Dillon*
> *Walker's Point Center for the Arts Board President*

Program Director

How you structure your program will determine whether one person does it all or whether there is a division of duties between full- or part-time people. In a stand-alone situation, the Director may be the Education Coordinator and Administrator. As part of a larger organization, the person who directs that operation may also oversee art programming.

The Director is responsible to the Board of Directors for all operations, including finances, personnel and administration. This person is the primary representative of the program and interacts with funding agencies, the media, schoolteachers, administrators and businesses and political agencies. He or she recruits and hires program staff, interacts with and helps coordinate volunteers and interns. The Director is responsible for handling everyday and long-term finances and all programming from class schedules to fund raisers.

If the program is running well, the Director is the one to take the bows. When there are problems, he or she must solve those problems and take the heat that rumors and bad publicity can generate.

The person chosen for the job should have a good reputation in the community, be willing to meet with corporate, private and foundation donors, and have the political savvy to deal with various government agencies and politicians. Most important, this person must have a passion for the arts as a means to reach and help children and a willingness to use that passion to inspire others to support after-school art programs.

Administration and Education

There are basically two aspects to any after-school program: administrative and education. Staffing depends on the number of children who participate, number of class sessions and the degree of community outreach. In a small program one person can wear both hats. Realistically it takes at least two people to run a program. Write job descriptions for all positions. Staff should clearly understand that the successful unit works as a team doing everything as needed. The Director may have to clean toilets and the Teacher may have to represent your program at public meetings or interact with funding agencies. These jobs may be part-time depending on the variables of the program.

Art Education Coordinator/Teacher duties include:
- Recruiting children
- Understanding student demographics
- Preparing lesson plans and class schedules
- Teaching classes alone and in conjunction with artists
- Collaborating with area schools and colleges
- Recruiting artists to teach classes
- Procuring supplies
- Organizing exhibits/performances of the children's work
- Evaluating program effectiveness
- Participating in fundraising activities

An organized person is needed to coordinate the program—someone with a background in teaching or art therapy is ideal but not essential. The coordinator sets agendas, keeps order, handles problems effectively and diplomatically, works with children and parents and does community outreach. The coordinator must be especially sensitive to the cultural and social conditions of the children and community.

See Chapter 5, "Using Artists as Teachers", to understand the rationale for and emphasis we place on utilizing artists as much as possible in the program.

Sources for program staff:
- Retired or active art teacher seeking part-time work
- Recent art/education graduate building a resumé
- Someone re-entering the workforce while or after raising a family
- Retired art therapist or one working part-time who needs more hours

The Education Coordinator Duties:
- Meets with school administrators and teachers to inform and show them through sample projects, photos, etc. what the program is about and how it benefits students and the community
- Integrates and reinforces academic principles and social skills through projects and program content

- Meets with social service agencies, churches and other groups to recruit children and volunteers for the program
- Contacts colleges, artist associations, local and state art agencies, and local and art-related publications to recruit artists to teach classes

Develop curriculum and lesson plans that offer a variety of ways to work on a theme.

A series of classes on Wearable Art is a perennial hit for boys and girls alike. Classes explore fashion trends, "crimes of fashion," and why we wear what we wear. Start dialogue with an introduction to fashion trends and designs. Invite a fashion-design professional, teacher or student to discuss fashion careers.

- Week 1: Design and paint t-shirts/tie-dye socks and shoestrings
- Week 2: Create jewelry from found objects
- Week 3: Design a space suit
- Week 4: Trace each child life-size on large craft paper and have each child decorate his/her image as a historic figure, favorite person, etc.

Integrate math, science and language concepts.

Wearable Art explores the chemistry of dyes and paints, recycling found objects, and environmental issues throughout the class series. Week 3 discusses living beyond Earth's atmosphere and clothing that would accommodate those needs. Week 4 includes stories about famous people in history or heroes the children suggest.

Ongoing Education Coordinator Activities:
- Involve children in project ideas and program
- Schedule, train and evaluate interns and volunteers
- Create project samples to give children a place from which to start
- Have the children create art for public spaces
- Promote exhibitions or performances by the children throughout the community
- Have a nutritious snack available daily
- Procure supplies: purchase or as in-kind donations
- Publicize the program
- Help with fund raising

Program Administration includes:
- Oversee general office operations
- Write and administer grants
- Supervise publicity/public relations/advertising
- Recruit and schedule volunteers and interns
- Do correspondence
- Help with fund raising

General Office Operations

Program size and budget will determine staff needs and the combination of jobs necessary to accomplish duties. You may have a full-time Director, a part-time Director and a part-time Administrator, or a combination of Director/Administrator/Education Coordinator. Using part-time employees is a workable plan as long there is good communication between all paid staff, volunteers and interns.

Whether your program is free-standing or under the umbrella of another organization, you will need accounting and banking procedures. Determine who will write checks for payroll, rent and supplies; do accounting and payroll taxes; obtain tax exempt status; determine operating budgets; and file tax forms. Finances are a major responsibility. A retired accountant who wants to stay active would be perfect for this function. The Board of Directors should regularly review finances and administrative needs.

Fund Raising

An after-school art program can operate on very little funding with volunteers, donated supplies and a rent-free space. It would be ideal to run a successful program and not have to worry about money, but normally the Board of Directors and staff must constantly raise funds.

Publicity and Public Relations

An adjunct to fund raising is documenting what you do, publicizing program accomplishments and publicly acknowledging donors. Everyone associated with your program is responsible for publicity and public relations as program representatives. Determine who is responsible for doing the following on a regular basis:
- Document activities
- Take pictures of the children and interview children, teachers and artists
- Keep in regular contact with local media about projects and events
- Record visitor comments
- Maintain a visitor sign-in log
- Inform the public about program successes
- Ensure that funding agencies get press coverage of projects they funded. Always give donors credit!
- Send donors regular updates on the program, participating teachers and artists, along with a photo of the kids at work.

They want to see their money used as intended—for the kids.

Volunteers: Invaluable Assets

Determine your needs and then let the community know how they can help. Do you need
- the walls painted or the tables refinished?
- someone to walk the children to classes?
- help making the children a snack on Wednesdays?
- help to clean a side lot or make a garden?
- someone to teach the children about gardening?

Notify churches, garden clubs, senior centers, schools and your local newspaper detailing your needs. Someone may volunteer to do a particular job, perhaps help every Tuesday with classes or answer the phone and take care of the mail.

There are people who like to do the things you need to have done.
- A suburban garden club donated money toward transforming a rubbish-strewn parking lot into an urban garden. Volunteers from suburban homemakers to college students did the grunt work. An architectural-design student made the plan. A garden consultant suggested plantings. Children planted seeds and plants and cared for them throughout the spring, summer and fall. Art classes were held in the garden. The children worked with artists to create a variety of sculpture pieces. They learned about the plants and weeded and watered them. They did portraits of the geraniums and rubbings of the leaves.
- During an art exhibit opening, Bill O'Dell, the husband of an artist, became interested in the children's after-school art program. Bill, a retired engineer, makes paper airplanes and gliders as a hobby. He volunteered to teach several classes on making paper airplanes and the principles of flight. The boys in the class especially enjoyed this distinguished man with a sense of humor and incredible patience. For many of the children, a male figure interacting with them in this way was a real treat.
- Some people have a particular knack for speaking to their friends or knowing the "right" people for fund raising or obtaining donated goods or services. A volunteer who is willing to assist fundraising efforts by hosting get-togethers at your center or at their home is a gold mine. A volunteer might regularly visit stores and businesses to collect unused cloth, wood, buttons, paper or any number of items to use for art projects.

Volunteers are invaluable assets. Use them wisely. Thank them sincerely and often. The Board of Directors might host an annual volunteer recognition get-together to honor all volunteers. Submit a photograph of the volunteers to your local newspaper to make the public aware of how the volunteers help your program. Other persons may be encouraged to participate in this worthwhile volunteer opportunity.

College Interns

Dynamic students who feel they can conquer the world are an endless source of energy. You may need to teach them basic tasks, such as how to properly answer a business telephone, operate a multi-line telephone and take messages. Once the interns catch on to your needs they can help do great things. You may get a student who will do only the minimum required, but for the most part, students like a challenge and want to do meaningful jobs. Some schools may ask you to grade or evaluate an intern's performance.

How and where do you recruit interns?

Contact all area trade or business schools, junior colleges, colleges and universities to find out if the schools require or encourage their students to do internships. At large colleges and universities, contact the department heads of various specialties. Send fliers for the career development departments to post on their bulletin boards. Invite the career-placement representatives from area colleges to visit your site to see how their students can help and gain experience.

Students who participate in internships find this real world experience looks good on resumés and can be a source for letters of recommendation to future employers. Some students decide to change career paths after their internship experience or become more dedicated to the path they have chosen.

The children benefit from meeting an assortment of young people from various walks of life who are studying a wide array of subjects and are very hopeful about their futures. Students studying art history, fine and applied arts, education, marketing, journalism, business and other majors all learn about a not-for-profit neighborhood art center. They experience a neighborhood they might not otherwise visit.

Middle-class interns meet children and learn about lives, frustrations and fears that differ from their own. The students and the children learn they have much in common. They learn to understand and respect each other by sharing their differences.

With a bare-bones paid staff, interns are an invaluable resource. The interns learn about the mundane and the exhilarating elements of the art world as well as the nuances of different cultures and communities.

Interns usually are not paid but often receive course credit for the time spent in the internship. If students expect credit, they will spend time at the center equal to what the course work would demand. For example, to obtain three hours of credit, a student would have to work at the center from six-to-ten hours per week throughout the semester, based upon college requirements.

Interns from any major of study, including art, art history, art education, education, business, marketing, public relations, journalism, engineering, foreign languages (especially appropriate to your population needs), architecture, landscape design, biology, botany or history can benefit your program. Trades such as carpentry and painting are also useful. Be creative. Allow them to be creative. This is also an opportunity for the children to meet a variety of young people while learning about education and career ideas.

To make internships meaningful:

- Direct and orientate interns, as you would all volunteers.
- Treat an intern as you would any employee. Communicate expectations.
- Find out what they hope to gain through this internship.
- Tell them about dress codes and any other rules that apply to staff.
- Ask them to commit to a schedule of days and hours.
- Discuss job guidelines and let them know they are part of the team.
- Encourage them to help with whatever needs to be done.
- Welcome their suggestions.

Intern Contract

Ask interns to sign a contract specifying what is expected in terms of hours, schedule, appropriate dress, assigned duties, etc. Outline what you will provide for them, such as written reports or evaluations for their school and letters of recommendation as needed. Keep the original signed copy of the contract in an intern file and give them a copy.

Interns often return after their assigned semester to help with and attend events. Student interns can become future supporters of your program and present a great voice for you in the community. Some interns may change career paths after their experiences.

Maintenance

Everyone needs to pitch in when it comes to maintenance and cleaning. For good staff morale, hire someone to take care of routine maintenance. Check with area high schools or social service agencies for referrals. Perhaps a parent or a group of parents would volunteer to clean the center on a rotating basis. Because a lot of physical energy goes into working with the children, it is best to have someone other than the teacher clean floors, tables, the kitchen area and bathrooms and to keep walks free of snow in the winter. Contact a social service agency about hiring developmentally disabled adults for such duties. This could be a great community service for them.

Artists as Teachers

Designing masks can be a cultural or social learning experience as well as just plain fun—mingling creativity with skill building. Chicago artist Arturo Barrera used hundreds of black wax masks set into twelve 4' x 6' boxes of dirt in his exhibit, *Bring Back the Spirit of Life*.

Each mask represented a Chicago teenager killed through violence in one year. The exhibit was powerful, moving and poignant. Philosophically, it was deeper than young children could completely comprehend but nonetheless moving and a significant warning to the children about the reality of life on the streets.

The exhibit also made an important statement to those who visited the gallery from less-violent neighborhoods.

Arturo taught mask making to the children attending the after-school classes as well as fourth and fifth grade classes from Vieau Elementary School in Milwaukee. The children learned to do lost wax relief: a system of using a mold to make a mask, shaping it—in this case to their faces—and then dipping it in hot wax.

The children toured the exhibit. Arturo explained why he created it and what it meant to him before they participated in the mask-making process. Although his artistic message was somber, he encouraged the children to make their masks full of life by painting them bright colors and decorating them with feathers, sequins and glitter.

Arturo tried to help the children understand the reality and tragedy of the streets as well as the other side of life—there can be hope and options. He showed them how making art is a way to express yourself and how art helps you deal with the pain you experience from the parts of life you do not understand. He explained how making art can instill hope and offer ways to concentrate on the positive elements of life. These philosophical concepts were discussed with the children while they made their masks. The painting and decoration they chose reflected their individual points of view while they enjoyed interactions with the artist, fellow students and teachers. The students learned how the artist expressed his frustrations and anger by making art rather than using guns or knives. He also demonstrated that the progression through anger, fear and frustration can be a shared experience. In the hands of the children, the black masks of death transformed into bright masks of hope.

Artists are capable of small wonders.

We need to find new ways to enable children to grow up whole, to allow creativity to flourish and to let them have a childhood. One way to encourage creativity is to make the environment stimulating, even entertaining. The easiest way to do this is to hire artists as teachers. They are free-thinking and experimental. Risk is often their byword when it involves looking at things from a different perspective.

Encourage and reward open thought and expression within boundaries and rules. Guide children, yet encourage freedom of expression and allow their imaginations to soar. Offer children glitter, glue, feathers, crayons, bits of fabric and other materials to decorate hats. They can decorate the hat brim and top or make an overall design using one or all of the materials available to decorate the hat. However, teach them not to waste materials, not to make an unnecessary mess of their work area and not to interfere with any other child's creation. They can have fun, experiment and be creative yet be mindful of waste and respectful of the work of others.

Artists generally retain their natural curiosity and talent from childhood. For most of us, this is diminished by reproof and negative experiences. Artists, whether formally trained or self-taught, can inspire children to use their natural creativity to envision and produce three-dimensional objects, poetry or music.

Artists can help build a child's confidence.

Artists take on new projects or try new techniques based on curiosity or inspiration. They encourage children to try something new and to continue with that process. The child learns that it is okay to fail when trying something new. What is important is to try again—taking a new path, mixing a new color, forming a new base of support. Each tiny step along the way is an accomplishment to applaud.

Inspiration can come from viewing everyday situations, objects or people. Showing photographs, posters, paintings and sculpture to children can inspire thoughts and questions. The joy of doing art amplifies when a child learns a few technical aspects. Having successful projects to show family and friends inspires the child to overcome the fear of creating. Creativity flourishes as the fear of the unknown diminishes. The child will see that art is everywhere, for everyone to do and enjoy.

Artists can teach children that there are many ways of looking at and interpreting both art objects and our everyday lives.

Marian Vieux has won national renown for wrapping trees with bright materials, including designer fabrics and surveyors' tape. She worked with youngsters in Walker's Point, an industrial neighborhood on Milwaukee's near south side, to wrap light poles, billboard supports and huge concrete highway overpass supports. Teenagers and neighborhood residents as well as those who passed through the area were amazed at how adding strips of brightly colored fabric to everyday structures made such a significant difference in the surroundings. The poles wrapped in bright designs gave a lighter and brighter feel to the area. Frequently the reaction was "Who would think such a small change would make such a difference?" It is amazing what a little creativity and vision can accomplish and what a positive impact art can have on viewers' attitudes.

The arts are a wonderful way to explore various cultures

The Mexican tradition of *Dia de los Muertos*, Day of the Dead, remembers and celebrates the lives of deceased loved ones using folk art home altars, music and poetry to honor friends and relatives. Families create whimsical or touching home altars using photographs of the deceased and displaying his or her favorite objects such as toys, cooking utensils, a tobacco tin or a special pair of dancing shoes. The altars may be a simple remembrance through photos and flowers placed on a small shelf or on top of a television set. Other altars may include flowers, favorite foods and beverages of the loved one as well as photographs and colorful paper decorations that fill a whole room. Lively music, skeletons decorated as musicians or in other whimsical garb and poems about the individual or family are all part of the *Dia de los Muertos* celebration. This tradition celebrates the belief in an existence after death.

Many artists use everyday materials to create their art. Art is not defined by the expense of the materials but the originality and imagination of its creator. Using found objects or materials from everyday life, even those with limited monetary resources can make art. Artists out of vision or circumstances have created notable pieces from broken glass, pebbles on beaches, discarded cardboard and even chicken bones.

Presenting a child with a variety of art forms stimulates the child to open his or her mind to inquiry. Artists can inspire children to be sensitive to the moment. We are not always happy and carefree. However, an artist who is sensitive to a child's troubles and feelings can encourage the child to work through sadness or torment through art.

Surrounded by art, we enrich our souls.

While attending after-school and summer art sessions for several years, Chris Vega had frequent encounters with a variety of artists. When asked how he believes these experiences influenced his life, he is candid in saying that art has become a part of his life. He decorates his room with art he buys at Goodwill stores and posters he collects as well as with his own art. He feels his room is his sanctuary and an eclectic mix of two- and three-dimensional pieces that reflect his personality. He makes art as gifts for his relatives.

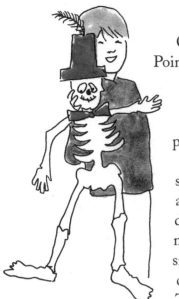

Chris credits the artists he met and worked with at Walker's Point Center for the Arts after-school program for giving him the courage to be himself through his art. He took as many art classes as possible in high school, even though he plans a career in the business world. Chris learned to use art to escape the pressures of school and teenage anguish.

Chris recalled that one of his most memorable projects was a series of printmaking classes. Barbara Manger, a professional artist who teaches at area colleges and universities, has her studio near the Center. She taught a variety of basic printmaking methods at the Center. She also walked students to her studio in small groups so they could see where she does her work. The children were amazed to be in the studio of a professional artist. They did not know people did this type of work right in their neighborhood. They saw her finished work and work in progress and her press and tools. They were given the opportunity to make prints step-by-step in this professional setting.

The prints the children made were so delightful that they were reproduced in bright colors in a note-card format and sold in packs of five to raise funds for the after-school art program.

"I remember the dark brown eyes and the chubby fingers digging into paper cups I had filled with cereal, raisins and M &Ms. In the gray twilight the children stood, chewed and gazed down from my third-story studio window as though they had never before seen their neighborhood. Then, with reserve and quiet I rarely see in children, they listened to me explain how to cut the small linoleum blocks and how we would print them on my press after rolling the blocks with brightly colored ink. They seemed pleased to be using real cutting tools and took great care to follow the precautions I gave them. They eased into this new task, their conversations swinging easily between English and Spanish.

"I watched their little hands turning the large wheel of my press and then excitedly lift back the paper from the block, revealing a reversed image. The crooked truck on a hill, a smiling big-faced sun, a jumping figure with wide-flung arms all appeared as mirror images of the original drawings. Although I had explained and demonstrated this, they were astounded. When each child had pulled several prints, they helped to clean up and then put on their coats. The older children took the hands of the younger as they walked toward the elevator. I watched from my window as they filed down Fifth Street toward National Avenue. One of the smaller children, Antonio, I think, turned, looked up and raised his hand in a small wave.

"I could still hear a shy 'Gracias,' and 'Thank you, Miss.' But it was I who felt grateful to them."

Barbara Manger
Artist

Art Therapists as Teachers/Coordinators

Art therapists add a new dimension to the role of teacher because they are trained to recognize problems not often verbalized and to develop solutions to help people deal with those problems. They teach and encourage life-enhancing skills. They use gentleness and tenderness to foster a feeling of safety and openness. With this sense of security, it is easy to open up and respond freely.

Deborah Schroder, an art therapist who served as Education Coordinator and taught after-school art classes, says that art therapists are taught to understand about the safety of paper as a form to express one's feelings. The children in the Center's Hands On program helped her understand this concept not just in her head but in her heart.

Deborah recalls a class where the children created self-portraits:

"We sat in a circle when the portraits were finished so that we could each talk about and show our brightly colored images. We laughed until tears ran down our cheeks when wisecracking Lourdes acted out her image's fancy-dressed, boy-chasing, older version of herself depicted in her painting. She kindly gave us two versions, one in English, one in Spanish. The art crossed all boundaries boldly and honestly. No translation was needed. When we regained some composure, the next child shared his image, then the next, and the next, until we came to tiny Teresa.

The image Teresa drew of herself was a pale, somber version of the lively, warm girl we knew. There was a stillness, an emptiness about that image that was deeply unsettling. Concerned about the risk that she had taken that day with her art, I commented only on the deep brown of the luminous eyes, giving Teresa, I hoped, the opportunity to stay on a safe level of conversation. The eyes were big and deeply colored in, she said, because they were full of tears—tears for a dead baby brother. In the art that day there was a place for everyone's story. The art said to us all that there is a place in the world for everyone's stories. Every story had the power of being witnessed."

Artists can be sensitive to a particular point in time and encourage expressing feelings that represent everything—sadness, joy, confusion or anger. Art is a way to experience the ups and downs of our lives.

Through experience and insight, artists can come up with a project for a class to do on short notice or based upon supplies available. Carrie Skoczek, an artist who taught many after-school art sessions, had an endless supply of ideas for classes.

Carrie went to a Goodwill store that was having a shoe clearance and bought high-heeled women's shoes, men's shoes and a variety of kids' shoes for 25¢ a pair.

She gathered glue, glitter, sequins, colorful feathers and bits of colorful fabrics, ribbons and yarn. The children selected a pair of shoes to decorate with the materials available and created a wild assortment of shoes to make any feet look like they were dancing or flying while standing still.

The children had great fun decorating the shoes. They learned that they could use simple materials to decorate their own clothing. They could turn worn items into usable fancy pieces or create whimsical art for their homes.

Artists such as Carrie inspire enthusiasm. They are never judgmental about the results. They generate energy in the children, who become excited about trying new things.

Art Teachers

Persons trained as art teachers combine the artistic thinking and abilities with the organizational training of a teacher to make a class or semester plan, evaluate student understanding of concepts and integrate academics with art. Art After School is not designed to be a technical art program but uses art to encourage creativity and expression and help build self-worth and self-esteem. Children are not graded on projects. They are not judged. Their participation is encouraged and applauded. If they learn a skill or facts—great! If they come just to have fun in a warm and safe environment, that is great too.

Barbara Niggemann, an art teacher who taught in public and private schools in Milwaukee, served as an Education Coordinator/Art Teacher, balancing art, academics and fun for three years. She knew the children were coming to after-school classes after a full day of structured activities. She gave them time to burn off their physical energy by helping her set up for classes. She listened to their stories from the day, giving them an outlet before turning their attention and energy to new endeavors.

She often began classes by having the children do stretching exercises. They giggled and then would breathe in and out in deep breaths to relax and calm down. Sometimes Barbara would read them a short story or ask them to share a story from their day before beginning a project.

With her experience as a teacher she had structure without the feeling of regimen. She managed to maintain the right balance of enthusiasm, administration and warmth. The children were happy to sign the class attendance book and help with set-up or clean-up activities.

Barbara spent time talking with each artist she hired before their scheduled time to teach to determine how classes should be set up. She made sure there were samples of the projects so the children would understand the focus for the class. She spent a lot of time at neighborhood schools talking to teachers, administrators and parents about the program. Whenever possible, she would integrate art programming to correlate with area school activities and curriculum.

Integrating Academics and the Arts

Mathematics is very much a part of the arts. Spatial relationships, proportion, form and balance are all concepts used in art. Children love to play board games. Some play board games such as checkers at home. As part of a series of class projects one summer, the children made various games, including checkerboards. They had to figure out the math to make the right number of squares and figure out the right size of the square to accommodate their checkers. The children found items to serve as checkers. They had to find 24 items for each checker game. The "checkers" had to be capable of being used as "kings," either by turning the object over or allowing it to carry a "crown."

Children received pre-cut wooden boards. They sanded the edges of the boards to make them smooth and then painted the boards with checkerboard squares. Some chose the traditional red and black, while others used pink and blue, white and yellow, or green and blue. Some children collected flat pebbles to use as their checkers. They painted one side of each pebble and then flipped it when it was "crowned." The children collected a variety of items to use as checkers, from buttons to bottle caps, cut-out cardboard squares or circles, and wheels from broken toy cars.

Some boards were a little askew because all the lines did not match up exactly, but that was O.K. Art is forgiving. When children make something and it does not turn out the way they want it, they can start again with a little help to overcome the mistakes made the first time.

Teacher/Education Coordinator Characteristics

More important than a person's credentials as an educator is the ability to relate to children who come from homes that put them at risk or do not provide a nurturing environment.

Children need adults who care about them yet give them the mental and physical space to be their own people. Children do not need smothering. They need encouragement to be self-sufficient and find their own identities. They need respect for their feelings and a sense of belonging. Being innovative, flexible, respectful, honest and enthusiastic are all traits that are important for an effective teacher/coordinator.

Art After School projects and programming can be simple yet incredibly effective if those people interacting with the children have as their priority a caring and understanding relationship. Adults who foster individual growth in a safe atmosphere that allows each child to blossom at his or her own pace are more effective than a fancy room with cold adults who require children to do boring tasks judged at each step of the process.

> *"The children enjoyed and appreciated the opportunity to work on projects and use a variety of tools—they often don't verbalize their feelings, but they do smile a lot. The first time I worked with the Hands On program I wasn't sure if the kids were getting anything out of the sculpture project we were doing. I didn't realize how much they were enjoying themselves until the series of classes was almost finished—they all indicated their disappointment when the project was over.*
>
> *I guess when you think about it, the kids don't have to come to Hands On. The fact that they come to the Center when they could be watching television or hanging out with their friends shows that they choose to be there and want to be there. The fact that they show up indicates the program is needed and is important to them."*
>
> *Mark Lawson*
> *Artist*

40

chapter 6

A Typical After-School Art Class

Watching children burst into class with enthusiasm and anticipation is truly heart warming. They depend on an environment that is welcoming, safe, creative, fun and relaxed for a few hours after school.

Art After School sessions allow children to be themselves without fearing judgments about their abilities, who they are or where they come from. Personally greeting each child with a smile or a hug sets the tone for the program by establishing a mutual relationship of caring and respect.

The Education Coordinator can be part-time and the primary teacher as well as the recruiter of professional artists who teach, the scheduler of classes and the one who maintains relationships with area schools and other duties. We were fortunate to work with a number of people from a variety of backgrounds who filled this role over the years.

Although each Education Coordinator has his or her unique way of organizing and carrying out the program, we use as an example a class model developed by Barbara Niggemann. Barbara did an excellent job combining her professional experience as a teacher in public and private schools, her artistic talents, personal warmth and joy of life into a successful art after-school format. Barbara was able to greet the children and make them feel welcome because she spent a lot of time coordinating all the personnel requirements and materials before the children arrived.

Plan Ahead

To make a class plan, talk to teachers in the children's schools in order to coordinate art and academics, to look at seasonal activities, budgets and available supplies and to hire artists to teach classes. Determine what projects have been funded and when they need to be completed. Then you are ready to develop a long-term plan with three parts.

1. **Make a three-to-six month class plan so that you can:**
   - Coordinate programming schedules with area schools to plan for after-school and school vacation periods, as well as other school collaborations.
   - Organize projects for which you have specific funding
   - Schedule projects that build upon each other
   - Have artists sign contracts agreeing on project, time, fees and who supplies what materials for the project
   - Coordinate volunteers and interns
   - Schedule the use of space, equipment and supplies
2. **Do a specific plan for at least one month of classes and:**
   - Make samples of the upcoming projects to show students, teachers and the public
   - Prepare fliers for the classes in English and any other language(s) required to communicate with children in your area
   - Distribute fliers and talk to teachers, parent groups or other contacts to make sure they understand what the classes will entail
3. **Obtain all needed supplies well in advance of the project and keep a stockpile of basic necessities such as:**
   - Old shirts to use as smocks
   - Rags and paper towels for clean up
   - Newspapers to protect tables and floors
   - Empty, clean soup or coffee cans and plastic margarine tubs for rinsing brushes or storing paint, glitter and other supplies
   - White glue, tape
   - Scissors, paint, brushes, pencils, markers and other basic supplies

Here they come!

After a full day of academics, the children burst with exuberance as they enter the center. Have someone greet each child as he or she enters. Welcome any parents that come to the class and invite them to join in the activities.

Designate an area for jackets and backpacks. Children should sign in for each class so you know who is attending and also can document attendance for funding agencies. The children need a few minutes to talk to adults and fellow students about their school day, but then they each must help prepare for the day's activities.

Instructors/artists are expected to be prepared and organized for each class. Do as much preparation work as possible before the children arrive. Cover the tables with newspaper if you are going to use paints. Have supplies divided among the tables or groups.

Barbara would take a few minutes at the beginning of class for the group to do mini-exercises or she would read them a short story. Weather permitting, an outdoor activity in the garden was fun for the kids as well as for the instructor/artist.

At the Center, after the children are given instructions and shown the samples, the adults personally interact with each child through conversation and encouragement. Sometimes the whole group might engage in a discussion about something totally unrelated to the art project their hands are busy creating. The artist/teacher might encourage discussion about the materials used, the reason for a particular project and other concerns to reinforce academic components.

Barbara and other coordinators often played music while the children worked on their projects. The children enjoyed hearing a variety of music ranging from classical to jazz.

About a half-hour before each session ended, they would talk about what they did, if they liked it, what they would do with their creation, etc. The children were all asked to help clean up, including collecting scissors and markers or dumping dirty paint water in the sink.

It is also wise to have a long-term, ongoing project available for the children to work on when they finish projects faster than anticipated. Education Coordinator Susi Watts made a large loom of yarn on a wall. When children finished working on projects or needed a break for a few minutes, they would go over to the wall hanging and select from a basket of ribbons, raffia, paper strips and other materials to weave into the wall hanging. It took many months for the weaving to be completed and it became quite a work of art made by many hands, young and old.

We suggest having available new children's books for the children to read. Children were given a book during the week of their birthday. Building blocks, puzzles, games and Lego sets were also available before and after class. Legos were their favorite.

A simple, nutritious snack was provided during or after each class. A modest menu of milk or juice with graham crackers and fruit, peanut butter and jelly sandwiches or cheese and crackers is always appreciated. For several children the snack was their dinner, so we tried to have healthful items.

Before the children left they were reminded about upcoming sessions and special projects. Someone would help them with their coats and backpacks and see that they could easily carry their creations home.

Mexican-Style Tinwork Class

Using tin to make decorative objects is fun. Cut out simple tin shapes to decorate or to make objects such as picture frames, candle holders, etc. depending on the ages of those participating. This is a good project for children and adults to do together.

Supplies Needed:
- Roll(s) of thin tin—quantity depends on how many squares or items made
- Burnishing tools—wooden skewers, crochet needles, dull pencils, etc.
- Colorful markers
- Colorful yarn, raffia or string
- Scissors
- Feathers, glitter, bangles or sequins to be added with white glue

1. Purchase tin at an art supply store or order it through a national art supply catalogue. Ask art teachers or the education department at museums for sources of supplies. Suppliers are listed in the Resources Available Chapter.

2. When ordering supplies, check that the item is in stock and not on backorder. Verify when it will be shipped and when you can expect it. Order supplies well in advance of the project date to have time to make samples and practice with materials you may not be familiar with before embarking on activities with the children.

3. Cut tin with sharp scissors. Pre-cut enough squares, circles or other shapes for each child and extra pieces for them to work on. Cut squares at least 6"x 6". Have each child plan a design and then burnish it into the tin. Color the tin with marking pens. Use a hand-held hole-punch to create a design if desired. Use one hole to loop yarn, string or raffia to hang the piece.

Suggested Tinwork Projects
- Ornaments at Christmas time
- Farm animal, jungle animal or pet mobiles
- A sun, planets and moons to make a solar system
- A family mobile as a family tree
- Several small pieces of tin that make a necklace
- Colorful tin shapes on trees any time of year. Watch them glimmer in the sun and dance in the wind
- Tin picture frames with simple designs. Take photos of each child or the group to put in the frame.
- Frames for the children's artwork or inexpensive mirrors
- A box shape of folded tin to hold a candle. Punch holes in the sides to make luminaria.

For a class with a Mexican theme, start class by playing a tape of Mexican music. Invite the children to learn the Mexican hat dance. Show them pictures of Mexican tinwork from a book and tell them how this art form developed in Mexico. Ask the children how tin is used in our everyday lives.

Children can do several tin pieces in a short time. Have them make a few extra pieces to display at your facility or use as thank you gifts. For a snack, serve nachos (cheese melted over tortilla chips) or tortilla chips and mild salsa, mangoes and other tropical fruit cut into chunks. Also serve a tropical juice drink.

Planning a Project

Weekly staff meetings are opportunities to share information on artistic programming, education activities, scheduling needs, etc. It is also a time to share ideas and solve problems. All paid staff as well as interns, volunteers, and even maintenance people attend staff meetings. This diverse group always evokes a whirlwind of creative ideas. Discussions get animated. Ideas fly from the mundane to the absurd. Eventually they are fine-tuned into workable plans and solutions. The only problem with these lively exchanges is that they generate too many good ideas!

Each fall we would plan our next year of programming. One year we heard about a program in another city in which a major retail chain funded a pinhole camera photography project. We discussed this idea at a weekly staff meeting and took the photography idea a few steps further than the other group since the Center's Director knew Al Balinsky, a photography instructor at the Milwaukee Institute of Art & Design (MIAD). Al grew up street-wise in Brooklyn and traveled extensively, taking wonderful photos of people, places and things that captured the flavor and culture of each place. Al's free spirit gives him the sensitivity and spontaneity to work with children of diverse circumstances and cultural backgrounds. Al rides a Harley Davidson motorcycle that also appeals to young people.

Al was interested in and available to do a photography project with children and teenagers. He suggested a timeline and criteria, including:

- Limiting class size to 12 students
- Including an assistant to help the children in the MIAD darkroom
- Limiting the project to a 3-to-4 week period
- Scheduling classes for several hours Monday through Friday
- Enabling children to go to MIAD to develop film and print photos
- Offering an inexpensive point-and-shoot 35mm camera for each child to use
- Providing at least 100 rolls of black-and-white film
- Providing paper for printing the photographs
- Providing camera batteries

It was decided to include the students' photographs with our opening exhibit the next season. Money was included in the budget for enlarging the photographs and mounting them for display.

Details. Details. Details

Once we formulated the concept, we had to work out the details. Every project involves details, frustrations and turns in the road to completion. Some people may view this as overwhelming and give up; we faced each obstacle as a challenge to overcome.

The project was titled *Our Global Community* because of the diverse backgrounds of the children who would be photographing a community of residents representing many parts of the world.

The biggest challenge to any project is finding the money to fund it. MIAD agreed to donate use of its darkroom and chemicals for the photo processing. We estimated their contribution to be worth at least $2,000 as an in-kind donation. We needed to raise money to pay Al and his assistant a stipend for their time and to buy cameras, film and photographic paper. We had to pay staff to write proposals, research donors of materials, recruit children to participate, do the paperwork associated with permission slips and parent/guardian approvals, organize staff time and interns to assist with students and pick up supplies while serving as the base of operations for the project.

We had to assess all the costs and variables in order to write a realistic proposal to the potential funder of the camera project. According to their grant guidelines, we appeared to fit their criteria. We had 30 days to submit a proposal.

Staff and interns got busy immediately writing more than two dozen letters to national and local firms associated with photography—including manufacturers, suppliers and retail stores for cameras and photography supplies. We hoped to get cameras donated that were scratch-and-dent returns and film donations or a price break on buying film and paper. Each letter explained the project, who it targeted and what we hoped to accomplish. After one week we followed up with telephone calls.

We learned that when you deal with a local store that is part of a national retail chain, the local manager may need authorization from the regional or national office to give special discounts or prices. A local Best Buy store manager suggested we contact their corporate office. The national office was very helpful. After an initial telephone call to discuss our project and need for cameras, we sent a letter detailing the project, a copy of our IRS tax-exempt determination letter and project needs and budget. It took a friendly reminder telephone call, but they did authorize the local store to sell us fifteen 35mm cameras at cost. We expected to have 12 students but bought extra cameras in case of loss or damage.

It can be a surprise and disappointment when prominent local stores will not even talk to you about a project. Put yourself in their shoes and understand that they probably get inundated with requests for donations to many worthy causes. However, do not give up, and make every effort to be pleasant, professional and friendly with everyone. You never know when you may need to seek their help again.

We were fortunate that two photography stores donated photographic paper and black-and-white film to the project. We then knew how much paper and film to buy and what we would get donated as in-kind. We wrote the proposal and sent it to the prospective funding source before the submission deadline of October 15.

Never assume anything

Just because you have a dynamite idea and a great funding proposal, do not assume that potential funding organizations will feel the same way. You can probably guess where we are going with this.

Several months after submitting the proposal for *Our Global Community*, we received a very nice letter thanking us for applying but stating that the company had committed funds to other projects. We called to see how to improve our proposals in the future and were told that had we talked to them before submitting the proposal, they would have suggested we review it with one of their store marketing managers before submission.

Lesson to be learned: Before submitting a proposal to a funding body with which you have no prior experience, ask if you should review the proposal with someone on their staff or do anything else over and beyond what is stated in their guidelines. This way you not only establish that all-important, personal contact but also find out about special preferences they have regarding proposal submissions.

In this case we were so sure that we would get the funding for this project that we did not even consider alternative funding options. Big mistake. However, mistakes can be valuable learning experiences that lead to happy endings.

There we were, in the spring, with commitments for Al's time and his assistant's and time scheduled for the MIAD darkroom. People were willing to donate some supplies but we did not have money to do the project. We had students committed to the project who were getting excited about learning photography. We had a wonderful exhibit scheduled with which to pair the young people's photography. Disappointment loomed.

One day when speaking with a representative from the City of Milwaukee Department of Youth Initiatives about becoming a summer lunch program site, we mentioned our photography project dilemma. The representative said there might be funds available for youth intervention programs if we met the guidelines.

Al Balinsky (middle, back row) and several of the Our Global Community *students.*

An intern went to the Youth Initiatives office to pick up the agency guidelines. The program participants met the agency requirements that they be residents of a targeted area, come from households that met poverty income levels and be in need of intervention activities to encourage them to stay in school and away from drugs and gang activities. Two teens from another neighborhood participated by paying a stipend.

Learning from our previous mistake, we spoke with program officers several times on the telephone and in person before submitting the proposal. We were asked to revise it because it did not target enough students in relation to the amount of money requested. It was decided to conduct the project twice, once in the summer and then again in the fall, using the cameras with a second group of students. The expanded project allowed more children to participate.

The photography project was originally scheduled to take place in June and early July. However, because we applied in May and had to wait for the proposal to be approved, we could not begin until August. We had verbal approval in early July, but did not get our written approval until July 27.

Phase I of the project began in early August, which worked out well because it gave the kids a chance to do something productive with their time when other summer programs ended.

"The photography project this summer gave me a new way to look at my neighborhood, the people and the things around me."

Sonia
Hands On, Art After School Student

Permissions slips were obtained from the parent or guardian for each participant in the project. Each participant was given a press card to show with whom they were affiliated when the student asked permission to take photos. We wrote "Photographer" on Center business cards for each participant. People could call the office if suspicious about the photographer. No one called questioning the activities of the children.

Only one camera was damaged during two sessions of the project. After-school students used the cameras in later photography sessions.

A project like this offers advantages for the artist as well as the children. Accompanied by the neighborhood children, Al was able to meet people, gain entry into places and view sights he would not have access to without the children as his guide.

The children found the photography project an amazing experience. Student Chris Vega recalls,

> *"The photography project with Al was my very favorite. I could not believe Walker's Point could put together such an experience for us. It was like magic turning the film into pictures when we developed them. Al was a lot of fun and I learned a lot. I still remember the group. It was great!"*
>
> Chris
> *Hands On, art after school student*

Our Global Community was a most successful endeavor. Every participant rated it an excellent experience. Much credit goes to Al Balinsky for his patience while we raised funds to pay for this and, most important, his excellent rapport with the children. The photographs were powerful. The students captured life as it is around them. Some of the photos depict the hard reality of living among gangs, drugs, violence and poverty. Other photos capture the tenderness, warmth and whimsy that a child can find in everyday surroundings.

Our Global Community: Final Report

We are including the entire final report on *Our Global Community* as it reflects the goals and accomplishments of this endeavor. Program note: We did not receive funding for this project the first time we requested it from a potential funder. However, we eventually developed a wonderful relationship with this funding source, which generously funded other worthwhile projects that had a profound impact on the children who participated.

December 27, 1993

Rhonda Manuel
Department of City Development
Youth Initiatives Director
City Hall
200 East Wells Street
Milwaukee, WI 53202

Dear Ms. Manuel,

Enclosed are the final financial statements and project review on our 1993 Photography Youth Service Mini-Grant awarded to Walker's Point Center for the Arts on July 27, 1993. The project involved 23 young people from 11-17 years old representing the rich array of ethnic and cultural diverse families in our community today.

In addition we have included sample photographs that the young people took then developed the film and actually printed the photos themselves. Enclosed are samples of our mailing and program which gives credit to the City of Milwaukee Office of Youth Initiatives for funding this project and the photography exhibit which occurred after the first phase of the project.

According to participant Miguel, **"This was a great project, I had something to look forward to each morning. A reason to get out of bed."** Participant Sonja found her photography experience **".... a new way to look at my neighborhood, the people and the things around me."**

The effect on the community has been incredible. The students went into a senior citizen center and various small businesses. At first everyone, was wary and many declined to be photographed. However, when those who agreed had their 8 1/2" x 11" prints delivered to them, they were ecstatic and proudly put their photos on display.

WPCA and most importantly, all 23 students involved in the project express sincere appreciation for your vision in seeing this as a worth while project. The positive impact such intensive workshops provide not only benefit the young people involved, but foster goodwill for the community as well.

Sincerely,

Jane Brite
enc.
cc: Mayor Norquist
    Alderman Witkowiak

December 27, 1993

City of Milwaukee Office of Youth Initiatives
Youth Service Mini-Grant for "Our Global Community"
Photography Project

Walker's Point Center for the Arts collaborated with Milwaukee Institute of Art and Design Professor Al Balinsky to provide twenty three area young people aged 11-17 an opportunity to participate in an activity that they would not otherwise be able to experience. The young people were primarily from the Walker's Point area and reflected it's culturally rich and diverse ethnic population.

"Our Global Community" consisted of two four week photography sessions during the summer and fall of 1993. During the summer session, the students met with Balinsky at WPCA to discuss and learn about the basics of film, the camera and photography. As young people are, they wanted to just go out and start taking pictures. To encourage this youthful enthusiasm, not a lot of time was spent on the technical aspects, but the students were taught these things as they went along and learned to develop and make prints from the negatives.

Each student was given the use of a Vivitar 35mm camera throughout the duration of the project. WPCA was able to purchase the cameras at reasonable prices from Best Buy. Each student was given the use of a camera and one roll of black and white film. They went out into the community in groups of 3-4 accompanied by Balinsky or one of his college student helpers to photograph the people, places and things of the neighborhood. Each student was allowed to take their cameras home to finish taking pictures on their roll of film.

They turned in their film and developed it in the darkroom facilities donated by M.I.A.D. Then after printing the photos, the students discussed their results, the technical aspects that could be improved, photo composition, angles, contrast, etc. They were then given another roll of film to use the next day.

It was amazing with the spread in ages, backgrounds and interests how the students managed to get along, help each other out and cooperate throughout the project. WPCA must give credit to Al Balinsky who was extremely sensitive to each child's needs and personality. He was willing to go to the homes to talk to parents, guardians and others so they understood the project, the timetable and student responsibilities. Balinsky made the project educational and fun for each participant. He spent many extra hours working with individuals in the darkroom, driving participants to and from their homes when necessary, making reminder phone calls, etc.

WPCA has found that this type of intensive project succeeds because the participants are given the individual attention, encouragement and direction often lacking in their home environments. The students need to learn to be on time for class, make a commitment of time, learn to see a project through, even if it becomes difficult. They need to learn that it is ok to make mistakes, and how to learn from those mistakes. Not only do they have fun while learning, they also learn life skills that will help them stay in school and keep a job.

Several problems that reflect the home lives of some of the participants include students moving and not knowing about it in advance. This resulted in some detective work to track the students down. In certain cases Balinsky had to pick them up and take them back to their homes each session. In many situations, the participants do not have telephones in their homes, so when scheduling had to be changed we had to leave messages with neighbors or relatives who did not always speak English. Students had to learn to call the center to let us know if they could not attend a session or check project scheduling.

Also, because we used the darkroom facilities at MIAD it was necessary for Balinsky and WPCA staff to transport the students to and from MIAD. Each participant was asked to have a permission slip signed by a parent or guardian allowing us to drive them to MIAD.

An exhibit of photographs by the participants was on display at WPCA from Sunday, September 9 through October 23, 1994. The exhibit was very popular and well received by the public. Many local residents came into the gallery for the first time to see the work by the neighborhood teens. It is unfortunate that no one from the City was at the opening reception (invites were sent) to meet the participants and see the extraordinary work that they produced.

The exhibit of "Our Global Community" work was up when the second group of 14 middle school aged boys participated in phase two of the project. They also received cameras to use and black and white film. Due to the time restrictions of school days, this group met at WPCA on Thursdays after school then went out to photograph people and things in the neighborhood. They met again on Saturdays at MIAD to develop and process the film. This session was under the direction of Jim Holzer of MIAD, who served as an assistant with Balinsky during phase one of the project.

WPCA has found, and it has been substantiated by educators, that it is important to reach the young teens before they get entrenched in the gang or drug scene. They need to see that life offers many opportunities and options. The second group was very enthusiastic and plunged wholeheartedly into the project, because of time constraints their work was not as extensive as the first group, but they certainly gained knowledge and respect for the camera as a new way to view their world and took home many extraordinary prints of their work.

WPCA would like to acknowledge the gracious support afforded this project by Jose Montavo, general manager of Helix Photoart and Ilford Photo for the donation of paper and film for this project. Without the extensive use of darkroom space and materials by MIAD, this project could not have been undertaken.

If funding is available in the future, WPCA would be willing to repeat the project with other area youth. Instructor time, film, paper and darkroom facilities are the major areas of concern. The students really learn to work together. They learn to respect each other's work and viewpoints. With photography they can do a lot quickly, or take their time on a project. All students can photograph the same object yet each will give it a completely different personality, based on angle, light or cropping. For teenagers who need to see quick results photography fills a bill that other media such as sculpture or painting may not be as immediately fulfilling. When the students see immediate results they are willing to tackle more intensive or extensive aspects and build on their experience. They increase their attention span because they understand and enjoy what they are doing.

There are always teens who need a reason to get out of bed, and want a place to be beside the street corner, projects such as this open the young people's eyes and minds to the world around them. They know what is wrong, they just don't always know the way to make things better for themselves or what choices they may have. Besides the time spent productively in learning experiences and fun the kids get to know responsible adults who they can talk to. The instructors also serve as mentors who casually, as the conversations come up, discuss each child's problems, needs and hopes. This one aspect alone can make a significant difference in a child's life and is well worth every dollar put into projects such as these.

III. SCOPE OF SERVICES.

The Walkers Point Center for the Arts will offer a four week photography course for approximately 20 area youth. The program endeavors to expose the youth to the "rich cultural and ethnic diversity of their neighborhood, then go out into the neighborhood... to photograph the people at work and play in the community."

In accordance with these program objectives, they request funding for the following:

		Actual Spent
Administrative	$ 300.00	$ 500
Artistic: Professor Balinsky	1000.00	1000
Student Assistant	400.00	500
Operating	200.00	200
Supplies	500.00	534.38
Mounting fees	100.00	107.70
	$2500.00 Total Request	$2842.08 Total Spent*
Mini-Grant Award	$2500.00	
		*at least $2,000 in-kind

Amount sought for reimbursement: $2500

2

OUR GLOBAL COMMUNITY

Al Balinsky has enabled neighborhood youth to produce a striking portrait of the Walker's Point area. Working with WPCA and a grant from the City of Milwaukee Office of Youth Initiatives, Balinsky provided the teenagers with 35mm cameras and taught them the basics of photography. For most of the young participants, it was their first exposure to cameras and photography.

In an intensive three week project, Balinsky and the youth went through the Walker's Point locale -- into stores and businesses, churches and parks, and around the streets -- photographing the visual uniqueness and diversity that characterizes the neighborhood. They recorded people at work and at play, in the everyday world of Walker's Point.

The young photographers not only learned to take the pictures, but to print them as well. Under Balinsky's supervision, and with generous donation of facility use by Milwaukee Institute of Art and Design, the youth watched the magical transformation in the developing trays as the pictures they had taken emerged. The photographs on display at WPCA were all printed by the youth themselves. The process of trial and error that allowed them to produce such wonderful images was made possible by the donation of film from Helix Photoart and photographic paper from Ilford Photo.

The resulting pictures by Balinsky and the group serve as a striking portrait of the diverse community identity of Walker's Point.

WALKER'S POINT CENTER FOR THE ARTS
Milwaukee, WI 53204 414-672-2787

August, 1993

Walker's Point Center for the Arts Student Contract

I,_____, agree to participate
in WPCA's Photography Project which will begin August 2 for at
least three weeks. Participants will meet at WPCA from noon to 3:00
pm on Mondays, Wednesdays and Fridays. On some days we will be
walking around the neighborhood together, on other days we will be
given photographic assignments to complete and on some days we will
go to the Milwaukee Institute of Art and Design to develop and
print our photographs.

**I will take care of all cameras and other equipment that I will be
issued to use and will return cameras to WPCA.** The Project Director
is Al Balinsky and will be determine participation in the project.

An exhibit of photographs taken during this project will be on
display at WPCA from September 19 thru October 22, 1993. I will be
given selected photos I have taken to keep at the end of the
project.

Date:_____

Name:_____

Address:_____

Telephone:_____

School Collaborations

The logical place to recruit children for after-school programming is from area schools. Even though many educators recognize how important the arts are on the overall development of a child and how the arts influence learning, the arts can become strangled in education purse strings. Too often schools need to budget for security, truancy, disciplinary action and other programs just to keep students in school, stretching the education dollar well beyond academics.

Programs considered frills—primarily the arts—are slashed. If a state mandates a minimum budget for the arts, this may translate into "art from a cart" once or twice a month. The art teacher is lucky to get a closet for supplies, if there are supplies. Musical instruments are costly; therefore, music is limited to a choir if there is someone who can teach music in addition to another subject or counseling duties.

> *"Walker's Point Center for the Arts is a wonderful bright spot in the neighborhood. Kagel Elementary School students are very fortunate to have them only four blocks away. Kagel is a neighborhood school, so students have the opportunity to attend classes after school as well as walk to the Center during the school day for many unforgettable experiences. It gives children a place to go with a positive atmosphere and the opportunity to use their visual and spatial abilities, creativity and intuitiveness. They have the opportunity to interact with artists and see their work exhibited and get some insight into the world outside their neighborhood."*
>
> *Linda Barlow*
> *Teacher, Kagel School*

How do you approach schools?

School administrators and teachers are very protective of their students, especially when the children come from difficult home settings or areas that threaten them with violence, drugs and gangs. Teachers have to work very hard to keep kids interested and focused, and must continually reinforce subject areas because there is often little or no academic support away from school. These children hear negative attitudes about education from their peers. They hear that school is a waste of time for them. Too many kids turn off or drop out because they do not see any hope for their futures. Go to college? Work as a bank teller? Me, do what?

When approaching school staff, do not move in on their territory or tell them they are not doing enough or are teaching incorrectly. They are doing the best they can with budget, contracts, mandates and other restraints. Focus on how you can help them and their students. Remember, this is a collaboration, not a takeover.

Use Visuals and Examples

Make your presentation interesting by showing sample projects. Bring materials for the group to make a simple project while you talk. Photos, slides or a video showing the program in action will help your audience understand this concept. Stress the goals and philosophy of the program with handouts, posters and sample projects illustrating how art is used to encourage creativity, reinforce academic principles and build self-esteem.

Steps to Develop Collaborations

Before you make your contacts be prepared to:
- Explain how Art After School can benefit their students
- Suggest how to integrate art and academics
- Do a simple project with the group
- Display photos of children doing projects
- Show letters of endorsement from children, educators, community leaders and parents

Make appointments to meet each area school principal (both public and parochial), social workers and counselors to explain how an after-school art program can benefit their students. Ask for a few minutes to speak at a staff meeting or in-service program to reach all staff. Sometimes an administrator may not immediately recognize the benefits of a collaboration. However, a teacher, social worker or other staff member may be willing to try a collaboration with a class or small group of students to see how it works.

Hold a reception for educators at your site. Serve food. A lunch, after-school tea or early dinner meeting always attracts the curious. Find out each school's schedule and offer alternative meeting times. Schedule a group of teachers and administrators to come on their lunch break. Have them eat a lunch you provide while you give an overview of the program. Allow time for questions and a few minutes for them to see the facility—all in a half-hour.

An after-school session or early dinner meeting should last an hour at most. Remember they have worked all day with kids and want to go home.

Have each attendee fill out a form indicating:
- Teacher name
- School name
- Grade(s) or subject(s) taught
- Special interests
- Extracurricular activities at school
- Personal hobbies

Leave space for comments, suggestions or questions. This is invaluable information for future support, sources of expertise or advice on projects.

Talk to parent-teacher associations or other parent groups at each school. Meet with the president and request time to speak at a meeting. Find out if you need an interpreter for those who speak a language other than English. Offer to bring the same materials that you did for teacher groups. Visuals are great promotional pieces. Food is almost always welcome.

How to market an after-school art program to educators and parents

- Show them this book.
- Focus on how you can enhance the lives of children through the arts.
- Be prepared to explain the program's philosophy and structure and components that reinforce academic subjects through the arts.
- Stress that Art After School is a positive after-school and summer time alternative.
- Explain who will run the program, where it will be held, the hours and the lesson plans for the semester.
- Explain artist-in-residency and artist-outreach activities.
- Invite teachers to bring a class as a field trip to see how things work.
- Stress how the arts can help to reinforce academic principles.
- Invite parents to attend classes and stay as volunteers.
- Have well-designed fliers about the program to hand out at each meeting. If you have a population that speaks a language other than English, have a competent translator translate the flier.
- Bring samples of projects.
- Be flexible. Tailor your after-school art program to the needs of the community.
- Be patient.

Remember, people will be suspicious of another new program. Art After School will prove its merit over time.

A Principal's Conversion

When we first approached an elementary school principal about involving his students in artist-led projects, he was apprehensive. He referred us to a teacher who taught music and ran the after-school activity program. She was enthusiastic and brought the first groups of children to the Center to interact with a paper maker. We collaborated with the school on an artist-in-residency project with another paper maker. The school wanted the children to have the experience, but did not have space to set up a workshop for two weeks, so the artist and our Education Coordinator set up studio space in the Center's basement.

The artist did a wonderful job of explaining the process of making paper. The children participated in all aspects of the process from pounding pulp to finishing the paper sections, so engrossed in paper making that no one noticed the raw surroundings.

When planning this project, Center staff suggested to the principal and teachers that children who were disciplinary problems—the at-risk students— be encouraged to participate. They looked at us in horror. You want *them*? Yes.

The kids thought this a great chance to be out of the classroom. We explained the rules and parameters of participation right in the beginning and clearly stated that those who caused trouble would have to leave. Once they realized what the project encompassed, they were 100% cooperative. A couple of times limits were tested, but we reviewed the rules and they got right back on track. The children were free to create and experiment within bounds. They were thrilled to participate and were amazed to see what they had accomplished.

After the children finished their handmade paper pieces, we put the paper sections together in a frame to form a large collage.

The teachers were amazed at the enthusiasm of the otherwise difficult students. The principal arranged a formal art opening experience for the entire school when the project was finished and held an assembly of staff and students featuring the finished piece and the students who worked on it. They were invited to stand on the stage and be recognized for their accomplishment. These at-risk students stood proudly on the stage enjoying their first experience of positive recognition.

The apologetic teachers realized that there was hope for reaching these kids. They just had to take a different approach.

After the presentation, punch and cookies were served to all the students, just as at a professional art exhibit opening.

The mural is now on display in the school lobby. The principal, now retired, joined the Center's Board of Directors. But before leaving the school, he hired artists as part-time aids to work with troubled youth in academic support. Now he speaks about his experiences at an urban, economically depressed, multicultural, multilingual school at teacher conventions around the country and praises the arts as a way to reach all kids, especially at-risk youth.

60

Ventures with Local Schools

The Jesuits (a Roman Catholic order of priests dedicated to education) set up a middle school for Hispanic boys in Walker's Point, modeled after the Jesuit-run Nativity Mission School in New York City. An alarming number of Hispanic boys were dropping out of school at the middle school level or early in their high school years due to gang pressure and other negative influences. The priests started with a sixth grade class of 15 boys. The boys wore white shirts and blue dress pants. They came to school at 7:30 a.m. for breakfast and then started their school day. They received instruction in all subjects and had organized athletics after school. They went home for dinner at 5:30 but returned for a supervised study hall from 7:00-9:30 p.m.

But the school did not have anyone to teach art, so the administration asked to have the boys participate in art classes at the Center. The Education Coordinator set up class times for them and they paid a small stipend to cover her extra time.

The boys came each week with a priest or teacher and enjoyed projects and interactions with different artists. They especially enjoyed interacting with Hispanic artists who performed or produced Latin exhibits such as *Dias de los Muertos (Day of the Dead)*. During the second year of the Jesuit Nativity School, a new class of sixth grade boys began. We cooperated by adding a second session to accommodate sixth and seventh grade students in separate classes. This arrangement was beneficial for all.

During their third year, the Nativity School hired a retired nun to teach art to the boys at their school because the administration realized how important the arts were throughout their academic programming.

Rose Guajardo, principal of Kagel Elementary School, located near the Center, was at first tentative about endorsing the after-school art program to her students and parents. She and several teachers visited the Center, met with the Education Coordinator, observed class sessions and realized what a worthwhile activity the after-school art programming could be for the neighborhood children. She encouraged her staff to support the after-school art program, and through the years, the Center and school co-sponsored artists in residency and other joint arts and education programs.

Collaborations can range from a school's encouraging students to attend after-school art classes, participating in artist-in-residency programs, or providing the art needs of a small school program. Collaborations can be short-term for one project or long-term. An advantage of being located in an art center is the ever-changing visual and performing artists with whom students can interact. They learn about and participate in art experiences they would otherwise not have. Every artist who performed or exhibited at the Center spoke with the children about their work, conducted a workshop or taught a class related to their art. Some artists gave talks or performed for an assembly of students at area schools.

> *"I will never forget the afternoon we walked children to the Center to meet artist Francisco Mora, who showed slides of his work and talked about how objects and experiences from his culture influence his work. The children soaked up every word. Many of them were of the same culture and could see themselves validated as well. After seeing the slide show on how Francisco created his books, students had a chance to express themselves by making their own books. Teachers received autographed copies of books written and illustrated by Francisco for the classroom. The children love the colorful, animated animals and the words in Spanish sprinkled throughout his stories."*
>
> *Linda Barlow*
> *Teacher, Kagel School*

The phenomenal impact of children working with artists and making art, no matter how simple or complex, is amazing. Children acquire a sense of ownership as they watch, listen and participate in the process of creating. They interpret the art they see and experience, thus developing incredible insight about art they see and do.

Ulanda, a 10-year-old student, often quiet and reserved, became bubbly and exuberant when an adult would ask her about her art or the art work in the gallery. Her eyes would get big and her face expressive as she explained the art on exhibit. She was increasingly willing to talk to people because she knew she was interesting to the listener. Her self-esteem improved steadily throughout her art after-school career.

School collaborations are a natural approach for starting an Art After School program in your community. But keep in mind that the children have been in a structured class environment all day. They need time to let off some steam before embarking on a creative journey. Include activity such as exercises, yoga or stretching before each session. Periodically schedule time to read a story or have a child or two read to the group before the project or activity begins.

Children need a time to relax before plunging into a new endeavor. So try not to make the after-school art program an extension of the school day. Foster the flow of creativity and encourage personal expression in a free, non-judgmental atmosphere.

chapter 9

Neighborhood Involvement

Develop the mission for your after-school art program in light of the ethnicity, culture and spirit of your area. Walker's Point Center for the Arts is located in a culturally diverse, low-income neighborhood. There are numerous run-down and abandoned buildings and deteriorating factories. Some revitalization is taking place.

Artist Marian Vieux, nationally famous for her innovative approach to wrapping trees with brightly colored fabrics, received a grant to wrap street light poles, billboard supports, telephone poles and light poles in the area with bright swatches of fabric.

Marian enlisted the help of area teenagers through social service agencies and paid them a small stipend from the grant to help her create the wrapped pieces. She purchased high-quality, brightly colored and patterned designer fabrics. The young people helped her cut the fabric into wide strips and then wrapped the fabric strips around light poles, billboard supports, columns on the front of the Center and various structures along a main street. The effect was incredible. The bright colors and patterns were a pleasant diversion in the surroundings. The neighbors at first thought it odd to see a woman and a group of teenagers mounting tall ladders to wrap the poles. The end result of the wrapped poles had a dramatic effect.

The wrapped structures retained their crisp look for over a year. The fabric eventually was removed when it became soiled and tattered by the weather. Although the project seems straightforward, we went through considerable hoops seeking approvals from the city street-light and forestry departments, the state agency in charge of highway underpass supports and a billboard company.

A number of area residents, social service agencies, business people and the Hispanic Chamber of Commerce were approached for letters of support, endorsements, approvals and help. An area church provided lunches for young people who helped wrap the poles. The planning involved letter writing and meetings with diverse groups for over a year. In the end they all came together to celebrate the final effect of the project. The neighbors became even more supportive of the after-school art program when they saw how the bright colors transformed their surroundings and saw neighborhood young people participating in positive activities.

Street Banner Project

A board member, Barbara Manger, taught art at a suburban college. She has a print studio near the Center and would periodically teach a class on print-making to the after-school art students. She worked with them on preliminary designs at the Center and then walked them to her studio to use her press. The students created imaginative pieces. Some of their work was used to make note cards. We sold the note cards at a fund raiser and used some as thank you gifts to special donors.

Each semester Barbara recommended that her students participate in an internship with the after-school art program. One student had a particular interest in teaching students to silk screen. This evolved into a banner project through which he worked with kids to design and print banners. The banners hang from light poles along several blocks along a main thoroughfare through the neighborhood. Several businesses, residents and the local Hispanic Chamber of Commerce sent letters of support to the City Arts Council in favor of funding this project. Funding was obtained. The banners went up and proudly welcome everyone to the area.

A successful after-school program does not occur solely within its own walls. By doing projects that involve the neighborhood, you gain visibility and support for after-school programming. The children learn about the approval processes needed to do public projects. They learn to speak to and interact with adults who visit the Center and talk to them about doing art after-school. It is heartwarming to see the children speak knowledgeably about their art projects and freely express how much they enjoy making art and helping to beautify their neighborhood.

José the Barber

José the Barber is influential in the area. He has a dynamic personality and the opportunity to speak to a captive audience when customers sit in his chair as he cuts their hair. José was very impressed with the kids as they passed his shop on the way to the Center. He often spoke with them as he stood on his front step. They proudly showed him their creations and talked freely about what they did at the Center. José posted program fliers in his shop window and encouraged children to attend the classes.

José the Barber became José the Artist when he put together an altar for a *Dias de los Muertos (Day of the Dead)* exhibit. National artists created altars for the first *Day of the Dead* exhibit. Area residents who came to see the exhibit suggested we repeat it again the next year, using local people to make altars because this is a folk art based on family traditions. *Day of the Dead* exhibitions expanded to embrace other cultures and become an annual event.

José and Maria Chavez

José and Maria Chavez volunteered to organize the next *Day of the Dead* exhibit. José made jewelry as a hobby but did not consider himself a professional artist. However, after doing workshops for the kids and the public on Mexican tissue-paper carving and other crafts, he became more and more involved in art. José eventually became a board member and treasurer. Maria is instrumental in organizing the annual *Day of the Dead* and *Latin Christmas* exhibits.

Iris and the San Juan Grocery Store

Iris and her husband are from Puerto Rico. They own a small corner grocery store near the Center. Iris works long hours, seven days a week at her small store. She has to be wary of robberies, bad checks, shoplifters and other small business problems. She operates on a minimal profit margin, yet she was so happy that we bought food for the kids and other supplies from her that she gave us a 10 percent discount! Iris realized the importance of art after-school classes for the children and neighborhood. In her quiet way, she showed her support and appreciation for the after-school art program.

Art for the Community

A great way to showcase the work of the children and promote your program is to display pieces in stores and offices throughout the neighborhood and around your town, city and state. A changing array of quilts, nicely framed art work, cleverly positioned sculpture pieces, or photo collages of children doing art showcases your program while enhancing store or office spaces. Sharing art by the children and the artists is an inexpensive way to publicize

arts activities. Encourage newspapers and television stations to cover your activities whenever possible because everyone likes to see news about children in positive endeavors.

Turn Trash Cans Into Art Pieces

We partnered with Safe & Sound, a community-based, anti-crime initiative in Milwaukee, to initiate art programming for young teens at several Safe & Sound sites. We received funding to involve the teens in painting park benches. To get the teens excited about participating in art projects and teach them some basic elements of design, we had them paint trash cans. A local neighborhood organization received permission from the area alderman for that district of the city to conduct the project. Department of Public Works employees delivered two trash cans to a Safe & Sound site in a church. We carried the cans inside where they were primed and painted a solid base of blue since we were using an under-the-sea theme for the cans.

One afternoon was spent with the teens and an artist looking through picture books with ocean scenes of fish and other creatures. The teens made sketches of the fish or creatures they wanted to include on the trash-can scene. The sketches were displayed on a wall.

On the second afternoon, the sketches were laid out on the trash cans to create a whimsical display. The teens had a variety of skills. Some wanted to paint a fish or creature on the cans. Those less skilled painted the background, a sand bottom and seaweed. Even some young men who were at first hesitant took time from their break-dancing sessions to sketch or paint for a while.

Three girls and the artist added detail and finished the cans, which were taken to an area middle school to serve as bright and cheery receptacles for trash.

Need supplies?

Many communities have a weekly or monthly shopper newspaper that lists everything from rummage sales to vitamin sales. Place a small listing asking people to donate yarn, fabric or other leftover craft items. You will be amazed at what people donate. One woman brought boxes and boxes of craft items left over from Girl Scout troop activities. We used everything. Seek supplies and help from:
- Churches
- Senior citizen centers

- Social service agencies
- Boy Scouts/Girl Scouts
- Chamber of Commerce
- Fraternal organizations and civic clubs

Do not be afraid to involve them in fund raising and collaborative art projects. Have the children create a whimsical sculpture piece for a senior citizen center, post office lobby or chamber of commerce office.

One of our first art teachers suggested that someone be in charge of obtaining supplies because so many items are needed. Board members, volunteers and staff should be on the lookout for inexpensive items. You can make art from almost anything: buttons, pop bottle caps, nuts, bolts, cardboard and string. Oftentimes the supplies available will dictate what art projects will occur.

Neighborhood Associations

Investigate whether your community can partner with a neighborhood association to add art programming to existing after-school or community-based activities. Neighborhood associations are often composed of concerned residents, business owners, educators and religious organizations that through combined representation take an active role in improving and enhancing their neighborhoods. Area organizations such as these are invaluable resources to open doors and help you reach the right person in local government, business or education when you need information or approvals to do a public project.

Help Might be Right Next Door or Across the Street

Across from Walker's Point Center for the Arts is an auto repair garage. Several rather rough-looking young men work there and we were suspicious about the business. However, when we needed our cars started on a cold day or a heavy box moved, the young men helped us even when communication was difficult, since they spoke very little English.

One young man who came into the Center when we asked for help was surprised to see teenagers painting murals on the walls for an exhibit. The next day he returned with a piece of canvas he had painted rolled up in newspaper. He proudly showed it to the Director as if to imply that he was a kindred spirit. He was invited to join in on the mural painting.

Involve area residents from all walks and stages of life. Weave your Art After School program into as many aspects of the community as possible to strengthen your program as it becomes an accepted part of the fabric of your community.

chapter

Community Art: Murals and Beyond

Due to the large Latin population near the Center, we presented a wide variety of Latino arts, including murals, which are a significant part of Mexican culture. Murals can be used to decorate and advertise and to make political or social statements.

One version of the mural genre is graffiti. The graffiti prevalent in American cities is viewed as a sign of street gangs, crime, drugs and neighborhood decay.

Will was an intern while working on his General Education Equivalency at the Spanish Center located a few blocks from the Center. Will helped with office work and with the after-school children's art classes, where the staff recognized his artistic abilities.

As Will and staff became friends, he talked about how he and his friends did graffiti in the neighborhood. We hoped to encourage him to develop his talents by helping him and ten other teenagers aged 14 through 19 to progress from graffiti to murals. They were invited to do their graffiti right on the art gallery walls for an exhibition entitled *Street Talk*.

The participating young artists were recruited from various social service agencies. They were either still in high school or studying for their General Equivalency Diplomas. However, only three of them saw education as a means to escape an early death and the horrors of life on the street. Raoul started drawing at a young age and hoped for a career that would use his talent.

> *"I was around eight years old when I was looking at my friend and started drawing him," Raoul said. "I want to be an architect so I can draw and make money."*

We gave each participant a sketchbook, markers and pencils to make sketches of their ideas and do samples of what they intended to do on the walls. Their only restriction was to avoid gang symbols. They were not good at making preliminary drawings because they do not spend a lot of time planning what they will paint. Graffiti is a creation of the moment for the space at hand,

usually done within seconds —minutes at most—before police or others catch them. Watching these young people use spray cans of paint to create images and write their messages was amazing. They worked together on each piece. Usually each one did the part he did best—faces, background, detail or a large image such as a car. They worked very fast. We let them use spray cans of paint because that is what they were used to using.

These street artists were very accomplished in their technique and a joy to watch as they covered the walls with images. They painted the floor and folding wood chairs when they ran out of wall space to cover. When they did not like the look of something they had just painted, they would all step back, look at it and then agree on what changes to make. One artist would step forward and wipe out the entire image or change parts of it in a matter of moments with several swipes of spray paint. They used brightly colored paint to create most of their work. Black was used to highlight and accentuate.

Street Talk received a lot of attention, both positive and negative. Graffiti is a major problem in many neighborhoods because it is destructive to property, unsightly and a sure sign of neighborhood turbulence. Certain television and radio personalities took it upon themselves to berate us for promoting and glamorizing graffiti. These detractors never visited the Center to actually see the work done by these street artists, nor did they talk to the young men or Center staff about the *Street Talk* show.

However, those who did visit the Center and had an opportunity to talk to the artists had an entirely different impression. The images these young people created were filled with the violence that surrounds them everyday. They were not innocents. As gang members, they perpetrated offenses as often as they were victimized. What amazed those who viewed the images painted on the walls was the intensity of their despair and hopelessness. They felt that they had to belong to a gang to have an identity in society. Through that identity they felt safe, believing that their fellow gang members would protect them from other gangs and avenge them if necessary. Tony did a rendering of the Virgin Mary in memory of friends who have died.

Since graffiti is about defining territory and asserting identity, *Street Talk* was described as an exhibit that was like a boom box going at full volume. The words and images used in the many vignettes that made up the show had an "in your face" impact, illustrating the artist's feelings on topics that included love, death, religion, drugs, life in the city and police indifference. The show offered a voice to those not often heard.

The artists were pleased with the *Street Talk* experience. They enjoyed the attention from the public and media. Overall, the public was sympathetic to their despair and feelings of detachment from society.

After the show finished, the boys stopped in the office to see if they could do something similar to *Street Talk* the next summer. When planning the next season we thought, why not take graffiti to the next step—murals? Grant money was obtained to hire an artist to work with the boys to create a large mural on six 4' x 8' plywood panels. In this format, the mural could be displayed inside or outside and be moved to different locations.

The *Street Talk* artists were invited to do *Street Talk II*. Several participants from the first year and a few new teens, including three boys from one family, comprised the *Street Talk II* crew. They were comfortable at the Center and interacted easily with the staff. They worked freely and became very articulate and anxious to be interviewed by the press. The young people felt radio and television exposure and seeing their quotes and photos in the newspapers were very rewarding.

They were given free rein to fill the gallery walls with several images, including street scenes, cartoon characters and religious themes. And again, the Center was attacked for promoting graffiti. In fact, we brought in gang intervention officers, sociologists and other community leaders to give public presentations on why graffiti is so pervasive and how gang structure and values for these young people had replaced their family life and value systems. Center staff worked with the young men on more artistic elements and preparing them to work with artist Pio Pulido-Frankel.

Muralist Pio Pulido-Frankel came from Austin, Texas, to work with the young men on a mural. Pio felt the best way to get the teens involved in the project was to ask them what they wanted to paint.

Pio was chosen to work with these teenagers because he understands the conflicts of minority youth. He was born in Mexico City, the product of two cultures. Half his family is Mexican Catholic, the other half is Russian Jewish, so he understands the need to express cultural heritage. Pio believes all ethnic youth, not just Latino, must seek out their cultures because non-Caucasian cultures are often not portrayed accurately, when at all, in the media.

The Center Director and mural participants spent a lot of time driving around the neighborhood to find a site to hang the mural when it was completed. They had to find a building owner willing to allow the mural to be attached; more important they had to find a place that was a neutral area for the different gangs so the mural wouldn't be "tagged" (painted over or defaced) by rival gangs.

Pulido-Frankel had only one week available to work on this project. Usually a project of this size takes months. Before Pio arrived, the boys began preparations by interacting with specialists in Latin American history and culture from local universities to gain background information to develop a serious mural.

The boys listened to speakers and told stories they heard about their history from grandparents. Much of this information was affirmed and expanded upon in the talks and slide presentations of the facilitators. From these discussions, the boys were inspired to feature Mayan gods and Mexican heroes in their mural.

Pio worked with the boys to define the images and stories they wanted to tell in the mural. They worked 12-hour days at the Center to prepare, outline and create the mural. Pio taught the boys how to use paint and brushes, not spray paint. The result was an incredible depiction of ancient gods, vibrantly done in rich autumn colors of burnt reds, browns and gold.

Pio not only taught them artistic techniques and expanded upon their understanding of the cultural icons, but also instilled a sense of pride and self-worth in each participant.

While Pio, the artists and Center Director were hanging the mural and putting the finishing touches on it, they were taunted by various gang members who drove by hurling insults and challenges. Pio talked to the kids about how they could protect the mural painting against other graffiti artists. He knew what they were thinking when he broached the subject. He knew and they knew that as hard as they worked on creating this wonderful piece of art, it would be only a matter of time before rivals would try to destroy it. Eventually a girl's gang did deface the mural.

Several business owners called the Center, offering to hire the boys to paint murals related to their businesses. Unfortunately, the boys did not have transportation to these businesses. Although the businesses offered to pay for the work, they did not realize that they would have to include the cost of someone to drive the artists, supervise the project and buy paints and other materials. But the boys did earn a little money by painting signs for a few businesses as well as special projects commissioned by individuals.

The next summer we received a grant from the city Social Development Commission to hire local African-American artist Ammar Tate. He worked with primarily African-American and Latino young people on another mural project.

The grant included funds to pay each mural participant $100 if he or she fulfilled all the expectations of the project. The idea was to have the young people learn that artistic and creative endeavors can lead to jobs and also teach them some of the basics of holding down a job. They had to sign a contract that they would attend each of the mural sessions, be on time and help plan, create and complete the project. They were also responsible for daily preparations before painting began and were to help with clean-up before leaving. In turn, the teens were provided a lunch and snack and their stipend.

Fifteen students were referred to the Center to work on the mural from various social service agencies. In retrospect, this was too large a group of students for the artist to work with, even with an assistant. A maximum of ten would have been a more manageable number and allowed for more individual participation. Twelve teens actually worked on the mural. It depicts various African and Hispanic historical and cultural symbols. The mural is on display in the gymnasium of a social service agency that provides after-school and weekend sports activities for area youth.

> What did the kids who participated in the mural project think about their experience?
> *"The mural was a very great art work. I thank the City of Milwaukee for giving money. We made a great piece of art and it was a fun thing to do."*
> *Enrique*
>
> *"This project was pretty OK. I liked it because I had something to do. It was a very good art work. It was excellent art work. It was the greatest art work."*
> *Tanya*
>
> *"What I liked was when we did the mural and the t-shirts. What I didn't like was Cesar trying to act big and bad. Ammar was very nice."*
> *José*

Another opportunity for a mural project presented itself that summer, so we contracted with Ammar to supervise another mural at a local Catholic church. No spray paint was used to create this mural, painted on a building that faces the church.

The finished mural is a collage depicting the neighborhood's mostly Latino culture. It shows children hitting a pinata, a mother embracing her son, a woman dancing with a skeleton and a man making an offering to Our Lady of Guadalupe. Embracing all the elements are the wounded hands of Christ.

> *"Our Lady of Guadalupe is featured prominently because she is the parish's patron saint. The skeleton is a symbol for death, which isn't a frightening thing in Latino culture. We just let the kids create what they thought would be a positive image for the neighborhood."*
> *Eddie Gutierrez*
> *Youth Minister*

Kat Hendrickson, Assistant Curator of the Center at the time, tried to urge all those watching Tate and the young artists working on the mural over the four weeks to join in and paint a little. She reasoned that by including as many neighborhood young people as possible there was less chance of the mural's being ruined by gangs. She was also amazed at the number of people who stopped their cars and got out to talk to them while they were painting the mural.

This mural has been up for several years and has not been defaced by graffiti. It is a true statement for building neighborhood unity.

These projects were important artistically and had a physical and psychological impact on the participants and the community in that they enhanced their surroundings and built relationships between adversarial groups. For example, when two foot-patrol police officers came into the Center and saw the kids spray painting their graffiti images, they were awestruck by the skill required to do this and the artistic abilities of the young people. The policemen and the boys had a friendly talk, a rare occurrence. The policemen even bought a couple of the t-shirts the boys had spray painted. The boys saw the policemen as people, not just "cops." The police gained a little more insight into the fears and thoughts of the kids. Both sides gained respect through understanding.

Public Art Can Inspire a Neighborhood

Public art can be a trademark for your program. Projects such as these occur through the cooperation and support of a variety of people and organizations. Children and teens can participate in projects with artists who are either internationally renowned or local emerging artists. Church groups from more affluent neighborhoods may donate food and money for lunches and snacks for the young artists.

Mothers walk their babies by to see the artists at work on the various projects. Elderly residents can walk over and talk to the kids and teens. People meet and talk to neighbors they would otherwise not have an opportunity to speak with or would be intimidated by.

It took a lot of care and feeding of the teenagers. We learned to include money in the project budgets for pizza, fried chicken, soda, French fries, chips and hamburgers galore—and yet they could always eat more. We had to dissuade critics, juggle finances, smooth frayed nerves and settle little disputes. We were rewarded with terrific art and an opportunity to enhance the neighborhood. It was gratifying to be able to encourage and provide opportunities for young people who would otherwise be forgotten or overlooked.

One young artist, Juan, worked on several of the mural projects. He did a painting of Our Lady of Guadalupe on the wall of the Center that was on a

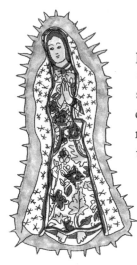

par with work by some of the graduate art students and professional artists who participated in the exhibit. Juan graduated from high school and went on to study commercial art at an area technical college. His decision to even stay in high school, let alone go on for more advanced education, is a rare situation among his peers and one to be celebrated.

Go Beyond Walls and Traditional Settings

When considering how and where to set up after-school art programming, don't be limited by walls or traditional settings. Investigate where the need for such programming is the greatest and be creative about how to fill that need to reach children and teens who would benefit from participation in the arts. Seek out collaborations with established groups that can help open doors and cut through political red tape. Prepare a concise mission statement and a two- to three-year programming plan to present to potential funding sources.

Art in the Parks

Safe & Sound funded a park bench painting project to both encourage teenagers to participate in the arts and give them an opportunity to show that teens can be a positive force in their community. Before proceeding on such an endeavor, obtain permission from whatever government body oversees the parks and equipment. We went through a local neighborhood association that steered us to the right person to obtain permission to paint the benches. Prepare a statement on the project purpose and a description of the decorative designs planned for each location.

It is essential to avoid negative elements or gang symbols. Simple designs, bold colors and patterns can have a positive impact on a site. The design should be appealing to those who drive by or ride the bus. Little details can be added to amuse children and adults who sit on the benches. Consider how the bench design will look during different seasons. Bold, bright flowers might offer a cheery look in the dead of winter; an ice-skating scene might provide a cool impression on a hot summer day. Nursery rhyme or cartoon figures add whimsy to a play area for tots. Benches near a swimming pool or ice rink frequented by teenagers need bold, colorful graphics.

Choose artists who draw well and can make designs in proportion with and appropriate to the benches and site. Ask artists to take time to teach teens about design, themes and color choices and the basics of how to draw and paint. Provide the best-quality brushes and paints you can afford for the project and cover the finished benches with several coats of polyurethane to protect the finish from the weather and everyday use.

People will notice the newly painted benches and want to use them as soon as they are painted. Put "Wet Paint" signs on the benches until paint and protective coatings have thoroughly dried.

Artists who have done decorative painting should know what preparation and materials are necessary before embarking on a painting project. Talk to knowledgeable and experienced people at your local paint or hardware store about preparing surfaces and the right materials to use.

Artists Working in Education, Inc. (AWE)

AWE, a non-profit organization, was established in Milwaukee, Wisconsin, in 1998 by a group of artists, art educators and those concerned about the dwindling art offerings for children in public schools. Initially, AWE collaborated with schools on artist-in-residencies at locations where children had minimal exposure to the arts. However, it soon became apparent that there was also a need for art activities for under-served children during the summer months. As a result, AWE launched the Truck Studio in 1999. The Truck Studio is a brightly painted cargo van loaded with art supplies and staffed by an artist/art educator and college student interns. The van visited six city parks for a week in each park on weekday afternoons. With minimal publicity, mostly word of mouth and the novelty of this attractive, colorful vehicle, children flocked to the van to participate in the free art projects.

Due to the success of the Truck Studio concept, the summer of 2000 saw AWE with three vans visiting city parks, summer school sites and non-traditional locations such as shelters for battered women and their children, a school for boys in detention, nature centers and public and private special events.

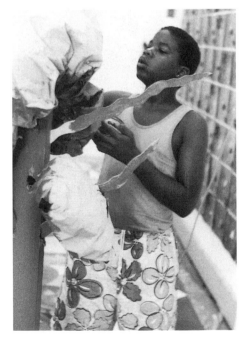

Funding and support for the Truck Studio came from private donations and collaborations with the Park People, an advocacy group for Milwaukee County parks. AWE received corporate support from the Ronald McDonald Children's Charities of Wisconsin as well an in-kind donations of the trucks from an electric contractor and an AWE board member. The Women's Club of Wisconsin was among private foundations that made major contributions to the Truck Studio project.

Analyze community needs. Find creative ways to incorporate after-school art programming to fulfill community needs while enhancing public or private spaces.

chapter 11

Safe & Sound and Art After School

Safe & Sound was developed by the Youth Crime and Violence Task Force, founded by U.S. Senator Herb Kohl of Wisconsin, Milwaukee Mayor John O. Norquist and United States Attorney Thomas P. Schneider. The task force is a broad coalition of more than 50 elected officials, neighborhood leaders, heads of youth-serving agencies, law enforcement chiefs and business and community leaders. The Safe & Sound Board of Directors represents all of these groups and implements Task Force recommendations.

Safe & Sound's approach is based on the successful Weed and Seed pilot program that "weeded" out crime and "seeded" three Milwaukee neighborhoods with positive alternatives for youth. Those neighborhoods achieved a 47% decrease in violent crime and a 21% decrease in crime overall in three years, according to an evaluation of the program by Marquette University.

Safe & Sound Mission Statement

Safe & Sound is a community-based, anti-crime initiative whose goal is to reduce violent crime by at least 20% within three years by bringing together a unique coalition of resources. Safe & Sound attacks the problem of youth crime and violence on three fronts:

• <u>Positive Alternatives for Youth</u>. Safe & Sound Safe Places give children and teenagers safe places to go that offer positive, constructive activities during the critical after-school, evening, weekend, vacation, holiday and summer hours.

• <u>Neighborhood Organization</u>. Community Partners go door-to-door in specific neighborhoods and plan events to share information and help residents support law enforcement and neighborhood revitalization.

• <u>Rough Law Enforcement</u>. Federal, state and local authorities cooperate with communities to target gangs, drug pushers and gun traffickers in the high-crime neighborhoods.

Positive Alternatives for Youth:
A Key Element to Reduce Violent Crime

Safe Places are housed in public and private schools, community agencies, churches and youth centers. 21st-Century Community Learning Centers are Safe Places in specific Milwaukee Public School elementary, middle and high schools that specialize in both student achievement and positive youth, family and neighborhood development. All Safe Places offer recreation, homework help, cultural and art activities, mentoring, personal development and non-violent conflict resolution.

Safe & Sound created a Program Council made up of Safe Place site coordinators and other youth-serving agency representatives. The Council shares successes and concerns and discusses strategies to help serve youth in their areas.

Safe Places are generally open from 3:00 p.m. to 9:00 p.m. on school days, some weekends and during holiday, summer and vacation periods.

They are an especially important part of Safe & Sound's formula for success. According to Federal Bureau of Investigation statistics, violent crimes by juveniles peak in the afternoon between 3:00 p.m. and 4:00 p.m., the hour at the end of the school day for most children. Juveniles are at the highest risk of being the victims of violent crime within the four hours following the end of the school day, roughly from 2:00 p.m. to 6:00 p.m. In light of these statistics, having Safe Places open and available for children can make a significant difference in the juvenile crime rate. Safe Places make a difference in the lives of individual children that will make all our futures brighter.

The Art After School and Safe & Sound Partnership

Safe & Sound teamed with Art After School because of a mutual goal to positively impact youth through after-school programs in high crime areas where young people are more likely to commit or be victims of crime. Art After

School offers additional strategies using the arts to achieve the goals of intervention and prevention. Safe Places are wonderful resources where children can start building strong futures. At the same time, they avoid gangs, drugs and guns that can rob them of their opportunities and potential.

Safe Places— Standards of Excellence

Safe Places are held to five standards of excellence, which are the evaluation criteria that each Safe Place must meet to be a part of Safe & Sound:

• Academic Achievement

Each Safe Place has academic programs in place such as homework help classes, academic clubs or tutorial services. Staff is also trained to identify children who need help with academics and encourage parents to participate in their child's education.

• Recreational Programs

Programs are designed to strike a balance between active and quiet, indoor and outdoor and structured and open recreation. The staff at each site also works to ensure that everyone in the neighborhood knows what's being offered and how they can participate.

• Personal and Interpersonal Development

Youth are given the opportunity to develop and practice social skills like making choices, resisting negative peer pressure and refraining from using alcohol, tobacco and other drugs.

• Collaboration with Law Enforcement and Community Partners

The Safe Place staff work with the Milwaukee Police Department and their local community partner to share information and promote positive interaction to help improve the neighborhood.

• Operational Standards

At each Safe Place site, the staff-to-child ratio must not exceed 16 to 1. Children are supervised at all times.

Art After School complements the offerings of Safe & Sound Safe Sites by illustrating how the arts can be integrated into a variety of after-school settings. Communities can help their children and teenagers by providing them with opportunities that inspire creativity and self-worth while empowering them to avoid the negative influences so pervasive in society today.

chapter 12

Fundraising Suggestions

Fund raising is a necessary evil to keep your doors open. It is important to determine the most appropriate way to reach the people willing and able to help you financially.

Individuals and businesses that offer in-kind donations of time and talent are invaluable; however, cash is necessary to cover the costs of operating an after-school art program.

Grant Proposals

Submitting grant applications to public and private foundations, individuals, businesses, corporate foundations and local, state, federal government agencies is the most common way for non-profit organizations to raise funds. A detailed step-by-step outline on how to research, write and administer grant applications and awards can be found in the next chapter.

Fundraising Ideas Beyond Writing Grants

We stress creativity throughout this book. Do not be afraid to be creative in your fundraising efforts so your program can survive and prosper. Look at what works for other organizations in your community. Find out what does not work. Be alert to what groups are doing in other cities and put a local spin on ideas for your organization.

We worked with a volunteer who was a member of the National Society of Fund-Raising Executives (NSFRE). She was an invaluable resource for ideas and had knowledge of local givers, who worked with our staff and board to structure fundraising efforts to target donors. You may wish to investigate the advantages of joining this organization.

You often have to spend money to raise money. There are administrative and salary expenses, postage, telephone costs and duplicating costs associated with sending out even a simple appeal letter. For each fundraising event, anticipate all costs, including paper products and cleaning, in order to cover expenses and make the activity profitable.

In most situations, fund raising is a mix of:
- **Personal**—in-person meeting or telephone call
- **Impersonal**—appeal letter or grant request
- **Social**—small or large gathering of people with refreshments and activities that encourage people to mingle

The best and most cost-effective fund-raising effort may be the salary of someone who knows the "right" people or, better yet, a volunteer. Find someone who has the ability to persuade people to donate money for your after-school arts program. The right person can make a few telephone calls or host a get-together to persuade people to support your efforts. Bring potential donors (representatives from corporations and businesses as well as individuals) to your center to see children participating in a class or project. This is often the key to having them open their checkbooks. Although the personal approach takes time, it is the most effective.

Letter Appeals

Sending an appeal letter to an up-to-date mailing list of socially conscious and/or affluent individuals, professional organizations and family foundations is a relatively inexpensive way to reach a lot of people quickly. However, the key is to write a well-worded letter that tells in a simple and direct way how these people can have an impact on the lives of children through their financial assistance.

An appeal letter does not have to be depressing or overly dramatic. It should describe an incident, a child, or a successful encounter that a child had through your program. It takes time to educate people about the needs that exist in their community. Some people may live blocks or minutes away from poverty, crime, hopelessness and despair yet never encounter or interact with those who live in dire circumstances.

Send appeal letters annually to individuals, family foundations, businesses or other organizations. Year-end appeal letters are effective because that is when most people make donations for tax purposes. Avoid being lost in the shuffle at the very end of the year by scheduling your mailing to arrive at the donor in early November.

Consider mailing out a spring appeal letter to fund your summer art sessions. Identify a small, select list of donors from friends or community leaders who would be appropriate for special needs funding.

Obtain donor lists from:
- Chamber of commerce members
- Local business associations, clubs, professional societies and young lawyer or accounting associations
- Donor names from playbills
- Published donor lists of other organizations
- Member/donor lists of non-profit groups
- A sign-in book at your center's front door

Mark your mailing list to send only one donation request to each donor annually unless you do a special appeal. Sending donors a quarterly or periodic newsletter between funding requests keeps them up-to-date on your activities and lets them know how you are using their funds. It keeps your group fresh in their minds and lets them know you appreciate their contribution throughout the year, not only at appeal time.

Include in your quarterly updates stories about the artists working with the children, and feature a special child or a project sponsored by a company or foundation. Include a color photo collage or drawings by the children with each newsletter.

Make a donor list and indicate:
- Date appeal letter was sent
- Amount of donation and indication if none made
- Other responses by the donor, such as requesting more information
- Date "thank you" note was sent

Prompt, personally signed thank you notes are a must!

Greeting card created by Hands On student

For donations over $50.00 indicate the amount donated in case the donor wants this information for tax purposes. Turn artwork created by the children into a note card, or frame original drawings as a special way to say thank you. Add a personal touch by having artwork signed by the young artists or indicate the name and age of the child who created the piece.

Social Events

Have you considered a garden party fundraising event? You do not have a garden? Perhaps your staff, board or volunteers can create one for the kids to use for a restful space as well as an extended class area. Let the children help design the space, grow plants from seeds or plant flower and vegetable seedlings. With the help of an artist or teacher, they can create garden art. Garden sculpture, painted flowerpots and wind chimes are just a few of the inexpensive items to create for the space available.

Always have a table where everyone attending a fund raiser can do an art project. Simple projects in keeping with the theme of your event will be the highlight for all ages.

Have two or three sample projects made up, markers, paper, glue, and other supplies necessary for the project. Projects can be as simple as folded paper to make and decorate paper airplanes, simple jewelry items or baseball hats decorated with fabric, paint, glitter or buttons. Have a staff member or volunteer help people begin, and limit participants to one item. People have so much fun they will spend hours at the table when they get the chance to be creative.

Put out a donation basket with a sign suggesting a donation appropriate to cover the cost of the project.

It is a nice gesture for the after-school participants to make small items as favors for the party attendees to take home as reminders of the event. Refrigerator magnets, painted flower pots and decorated bags with the name of your organization are all items people will use, and they also serve as reminders of your program long after the event.

Party Ideas

In keeping with an environmental and beautification theme, turn a trash-strewn lot, a small side yard, or walk area into a garden space. Develop a container garden using any vessels that will hold plants and soil and also allow water to drain through. Recycle clay pots, cooking pots, old sinks, bathtubs and even institutional-size food cans into interesting plant containers. Be creative and have fun. Use materials readily available and dress them up in whimsical ways. Be sure to enlist the children in weeding, feeding and watering the plantings. Have them decorate colorful containers for the front of your center or to put in windows.

Have a fundraising party for your garden in January or February. Decorate the space with large Mexican-style paper flowers. The children can create hundreds of them for the minimal cost of colorful tissue paper and a little wire or pipe cleaners. Invite parents, area merchants (especially those who sell garden supplies), garden club members, city, county or state horticultural agents or foresters, Future Farmers of America members, horticultural teachers and students—anyone with an interest in gardening, the environment or art. Serve snacks such as fruit kabobs and grilled hot dogs to conjure up summer.

Solicit donations of time, talent and money from area garden clubs. Conduct a plant or bulb sale to raise funds. If you have a county greenhouse, ask them to donate excess plants.

Create a display for the event that includes:
1. A garden plan created by a local landscape architecture student, area technical college class or teacher
2. A list of flowers, shrubs and trees for each stage of the plan
3. A list of tools, hoses and other garden supplies you need
4. Photos of the children doing garden-related projects such as
   • Planting seeds
   • Watering and tending the plants
   • Sketching or painting flowers

Ask people to donate and deliver plants from their gardens plus tools and other supplies, including dirt, fertilizer and mulch. Ask for volunteers to help prepare the soil and do heavy-duty planting. Volunteers can work with the children to teach them about gardening. Check with your county office about a Master Gardener program. Master Gardeners are committed to sharing their horticulture knowledge with the public and can be reached by calling your county extension office.

When the garden is glorious in the summer, invite those who helped create it to a gathering in this wonderful space. Have musicians from a high school or college or a barbershop quartet entertain while people tour and enjoy the garden space. Encourage everyone attending social events to support your program. Sell or auction:

- Artwork by the children or participating artists
- Painted and decorated flower pots, plant markers, garden aprons or brimmed sun hats made by children or artists
- Garden jewelry such as ladybugs, sunflowers or rose pins by children or artists
- Picture frames, t-shirts, decorated paper gift bags

Indicate that all proceeds go toward maintaining education programs.

House Party

Everybody wants to see a fancy, unusual or interesting home. Ask someone you know with an intriguing home to host a cocktail party for a select number of guests. Charge a fee that your audience can manage (indicate on invitations that all proceeds will benefit the after-school arts program). Allow guests to snoop around the house or offer guided tours. Board members and friends can contribute food and beverages (or better yet, get items donated). Have a table to sell art by the children and/or sell raffle tickets for various items donated for the occasion. Raffle prizes could be gift certificates for services from interior decorators, paint stores, drapery or curtain shops, garden shops, a handy man or lawn service.

A Board member at the Walker's Point Center hosted a party at her suburban home located on a lake. Besides enjoying food, cocktails and a chance to see the lovely grounds, guests bid on artwork drawn by famous people from throughout the country. Sports figures, politicians, movie stars and rock stars were sent blank 11"x14" sheets of white paper. Each person was asked to do a self-portrait, drawing or doodle of their choice. They were to sign the art and return it to the Center in a stamped, addressed envelope that we provided.

Several national figures and a number of local personalities returned their original art. We framed all the art for auction. All proceeds went to support after-school art programming.

Art Studio Crawl

Ask a few artists to open their studios on a Saturday or Sunday afternoon for an open house. Sell tickets with all proceeds going toward your program. The artists can feature their work and have items for sale. Participants can spend an interesting afternoon seeing how and where artists work, can contribute to your after-school art program and may find a special piece of art for themselves.

Special Events

Invite special-interest groups such as teachers, merchants, senior citizens and various civic club members to informational opportunities:

- Breakfast, lunch and dinner get-togethers
- Dessert meetings/workshops/open houses
- Musical and theme events, especially holidays appropriate to neighborhood residents
- Auctions of new and/or used art works
- Auctions of artist- or celebrity-decorated aprons/chairs/hats
- Sittings with sports stars who would sketch people for a fee
- Rummage sales
- Penny carnivals for children or adults
- Used-book sales
- Speakers on art, art therapy and music

People often feel more comfortable coming to a gathering if they know there will be a group or if they go with a group of friends or associates.

Volunteer to speak at meetings of professional societies, fraternal organizations and clubs, senior citizen and public service groups, education in-service meetings, etc. Come with sample projects created by the children: photos, videos, fliers and copies of newspaper articles. These examples reinforce the good things that participation in the arts does for children in the community. When people see positive results, they are more likely to volunteer, donate goods and services or fund projects.

We found that having the audience work on a simple art project while listening to a speaker talk about Art After School was a real hit. Pass out a handful of clay to each person. Ask them to sculpt their favorite animal. It is amazing how many adults pooh-pooh doing something creative—until they start. Then you cannot get them to stop.

Non-event Donations

A non-event donation is sought through an appeal letter. You send people an invitation to a non-event and explain how much money they will save by not attending. They will not have to buy a new dress, rent a tux, get a baby sitter, etc. In this way they save enough money to write you a check.

Soft Openings for Restaurants and Businesses

A soft opening is a pre-opening trial run of a restaurant or other business. You invite people to attend before the business officially opens to the public. People like to be the first ones to experience a new business. This is a chance for a new restaurant to test their kitchen staff and train their wait staff before opening to the public. They usually offer a limited or sampler menu at special prices. Your organization or the business does the invitations and publicity. The restaurant either gives you a percentage of the money taken in or asks patrons to leave a donation for your group.

Bus Trips

Bus tours to out-of-town museums, gardens or other attractions are an easy way to raise money. Collaborate with other groups to attend museums, theater performances, sporting events or other activities by buying blocks of tickets at a discounted price. Arrange for bus transportation. You can make a profit if you negotiate good prices. This is very popular among senior citizens. Senior centers are always looking for new activities that would appeal to their members.

Collaborations with Museums, Schools or Libraries

You are competing for the donor's dollar against many worthwhile causes and organizations. Collaborate with groups by co-sponsoring speakers, exhibitions and house or garden tours to share the work and profits. Through collaborations both organizations broaden the cadre of people they draw upon and can do an event that neither could do alone. Moreover, foundations, government agencies and other funders find collaborations between organizations impressive.

Collaboration Ideas

Have the children decorate bags as centerpieces or thank you gifts for another organization's event. We partnered with the United Performing Arts Fund (UPAF) organizers in Milwaukee by having the children decorate paper shopping bags with images of dancers, musicians and performance themes. The attendees each received their lunch in decorated bags signed by the child who decorated it. This was an inexpensive and clever way for UPAF to provide participants with a small gift that also showcased the after-school art program. UPAF provided the bags for the project and a small stipend to cover the cost of materials. UPAF repeated this theme for three years because it was so well received.

- The children can serve as greeters and hand out programs at a ballet or musical performance. It is impressive to see young people helping. Children have an opportunity to see performances they might not otherwise attend. Set up a table where children sell related artwork.
- Have children design invitations or program covers for area performance groups, churches, club meetings, etc. Increase awareness of your activities by displaying the children's artwork throughout your community.
- Collaborate with area hospitals, nursing homes and or restaurants to have the children create small centerpieces or decorative flower pots for tables or meal trays. In exchange for the children's artwork, these organizations can give money or food for snacks.

86

The important element in fund raising is to keep your costs at a minimum to get the best return for your investment. When you find an activity that works, stick with it, repeating it with a different twist each year to keep it fresh. When an event is successful, repeat it annually to identify it with your organization. People will look forward to attending and contributing to it.

Raising the money to keep your program afloat will probably be your most time-consuming effort. Knowing that you are asking for funds, goods or time for a worthwhile cause makes the effort easier. Seeing a child smile while working on a project will reward you for your efforts.

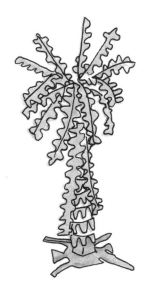

c h a p t e r 13

Writing and Administering Grants

Even if you are unfamiliar with writing and submitting grant proposal applications, you can begin by following the guidelines, suggestions and samples that we have outlined to help you navigate this necessary function.

Professional Development

Many metropolitan areas have organizations that serve as a resource for non-profit organizations. For reasonable fees, they offer classes on writing a grant proposal, preparing budgets and financial statements, setting goals, building a board of directors, targeting an audience and other helpful topics.

Frequently colleges and universities offer classes on grant proposal writing and organizational development through their community or continuing education divisions. Staff, board members, interns and volunteers can all benefit from these classes to learn about preparing a fundraising grant as well as how all aspects of an organization, from creative to financial, must work together on fundraising efforts and management.

To keep the doors to your program open, you need to raise funds. You will find ideas to attract donors and underwriters and suggestions for other fundraising efforts in Chapter 12. Be creative when researching funding opportunities: Think about in-kind services, staff training and professional development opportunities. Do not limit yourself to opportunities that only target children or education issues. Other groups to apply to for professional assistance and for staff training include:

- Marketing professionals
- Development experts
- Community involvement liaisons
- Business planning consultants
- Operations analysts
- Financial planners

- Legal advisers
- Accounting and financial experts
- Nutrition consultants

It is now common for foundations to collaborate on funding consultants for non-profit organizations. Most small non-profits cannot afford full-time staff in marketing or development, yet they need to periodically assess how to improve and update their performance in these vital areas. Foundations may target organizations that mirror their interests or may fund certain categories of non-profits during a cycle. They may fund arts organizations in some years, in other years education or children's concerns or social services. While they often have leeway to accept and fund worthy proposals, try to structure your request to reflect the guidelines and goals of the foundation as closely as possible.

For example, the Milwaukee Foundation collaborated with two private foundations to help non-profit arts organizations obtain marketing and development expertise. We applied to this grant coalition several times for funds to hire a marketing consultant. However, due to limited funds not all those who seek assistance receive funds during a funding cycle. We waited four years to receive funding from this particular group. You may have to apply repeatedly during several funding cycles. Eventually your turn may come. Review the following suggestions to see how to submit a proposal and present your organization in a way that matches the funder's goals and guidelines.

Grant Proposals

Submitting grant applications to public and private foundations, individuals, businesses, corporate foundations and local and state and federal government agencies is the most common way for non-profit organizations to raise funds. Putting together a grant proposal package is often the most labor-intensive means to obtain funding. Research funding sources through your local public library, college and university libraries, and state government sources as well as the federal government.

Most states have a directory of foundations. The directory includes information on foundations and includes the foundation name, address, contact person, officers/directors, assets, grants paid, number of grants given during a particular year, dollar amount per grant, limitations on use of funds, application procedure, recent grant awards, purpose and areas of interest (education, youth, social services, elderly, etc.).

Marquette University in Milwaukee, Wisconsin, publishes a directory of foundations for Wisconsin. The library has books and electronic sources to find funding opportunities throughout the world. The librarian of this section conducts periodic seminars on how to use materials in the Funding Information Center. Similar resources may be available in libraries at universities near you as well as through listings on the Internet.

The Milwaukee Foundation is a community trust representing numerous and varied private foundations serving a four-county area. Check if your community, a major city in your state, or a statewide organization has a similar structure for foundations that can match you with donors who have a focus compatible with your funding needs and goals.

Grant Calendar

Research funding sources and contact each organization to verify their submission requirement and dates. Establish a timeline or calendar indicating when letters of intent and/or applications are due.

Letters of intent are not applications. They are usually one- or two-page letters defining who you are and what you are requesting money to do. The funding agency's grant committee will review the letter of intent to see if you match their guidelines. If they feel you match their current focus, they will ask you to submit a formal application. This process saves you and the funding agency paperwork and time, but it does add one more step to the process.

A calendar will help you manage your time and expedite preparing grant data as well as your workload. You should not wait until the last minute to prepare a grant proposal; begin preparations as far in advance as possible. Sometimes a month is enough time. However, if you are planning to collaborate with another organization, you may need several months to discuss, define and prepare the proposal.

A grant calendar will also help you manage finances and your budget by showing when you will receive lump sum or partial payments for grant awards while serving as a reminder of bills to pay.

A grant calendar should list application due dates. If a funding agency does not receive your application on time it will not even consider it, no matter how terrific the proposal may be. List the due date one week earlier than required to allow for normal mail delivery, and build-in time to remedy last-minute problems. Send grant proposals via priority mail with delivery confirmation so you can track when it is received.

When notice of a grant award is received, immediately indicate on the calendar when all reports are due and when you can expect to receive funds. Establish a separate folder for each grant. File copies of all information associated with the grant in that folder. Keep accurate records and submit reports in a professional manner.

If your application for funding is denied, read the denial letter for hints about how to improve your application. When you can speak calmly, contact the funder's representative to ask how you could restructure your proposal to fit their current funding goals. Perhaps a personal meeting is in order if you haven't already met with them. Do stay calm. Be polite. Evaluate whether you will submit another proposal in the future.

The paperwork for grant applications is the lackluster part of funding any after-school program. Completing a funding application or proposal can seem like an overwhelming task. However, the paperwork is worth the effort when you get that check in the mail!

Some communities have adopted a common application to help simplify the paperwork process for those applying as well as for those reviewing applications. Most funding groups, public or private, require basically the same information. Yet you must tailor your presentation to fit their format.

There is no putting it off. Get a cup of java and then begin.

READ. READ. READ. READ.

Thoroughly read the entire application from cover letter through the last page. There is nothing worse than spending hours gathering data, writing a narrative to fit the space provided, and copying and collating hundreds of pages only to notice that you must send a letter of intent before submitting the complete proposal! Check the fine print. You may find that your Board must have on file a formal anti-discrimination policy. Even though your organization does not discriminate in any way, you must submit a copy of the Board's policy on this issue. What if your Board met last week and the application is due tomorrow? Do you send an incomplete application with a letter saying, "Oh-oh, we missed this requirement. Will send it along next month?" This is not a good idea.

Your organization bylaws may allow your presiding officer to poll Board members by telephone to take a vote. In this case, your Board president can write the required resolution and contact Board members for their vote.

DEADLINES. DEADLINES. DEADLINES.

Allow plenty of time to gather the required information in the appropriate format, to obtain signatures and to copy and collate all materials.

 Allow adequate time for mail delivery so the application arrives at the funding organization by the deadline.

Getting your proposal in a few days before deadline is impressive. Too often a proposal is hand-delivered, sent by courier or special delivery to meet a deadline. When applications are submitted a few days prior to the deadline, reviewers may be able to look them over and call with questions. They are impressed when a complete proposal arrives well before the deadline and appreciate the time to review it—something they cannot do when hundreds of proposals arrive all on one day.

For grants that must be postmarked by a certain date, obtain a dated proof-of-mailing receipt from the post office when you mail the grant package. This service costs a little extra, but it gives you documentation that you did in fact mail your proposal by the required date.

Ask a fellow staff person or board member to review the application packet before you begin to process it. Have this person double-check all materials, including the narrative, budget and attachments. State all information clearly and concisely. Sometimes we get too close to a project and forget that we are explaining it to someone who is unfamiliar with it. Assume nothing.

Completing the Funding Proposal Application

Once you identify potential sources of funds for your project, you are ready to complete the grant application. Have the following information available to complete most funding applications:

For the organization:
- Current budget
- Current income and expense statement
- Financial statements for past two years (if available)
- Projected budget for the next fiscal year, with a brief explanation of all changes under or over 10%
- Copies of your most recent Internal Revenue Service tax forms
- Copy of your organization's financial audit
- Staff resumés
- Board of Directors roster indicating occupations and professional affiliations
- Organization mission statement
- Brief history of the organization
- List of community-outreach activities
- Statement on handicap accessibility
- List of donors and amounts given
- Economic and demographic statistics of your staff, board and population served
- Board-approved long-range plan for 2-through-5 years
- Proof of insurance coverage
- Packet of media clippings
- Letters of support
- Photos of children doing art activities

For the project:
- Project purpose or goal (who will be served)
- Detailed project description
- Resumés or synopsis of project personnel's background
- Project timeline
- Letters of support for project
- Itemized project budget

Maintain updated lists and documentation of the above items. Have good, clean copies of this information available and clearly stated on white paper or available to print on your letterhead. Do not use colored paper unless you are sure the document will not be copied. Colored paper does not duplicate well.

A considerable amount or time and money does go into preparing background and project information for funding proposals. Staff time, consultant fees, wages for the proposal writer, costs to create financial statements, proposal copies and postage to mail the proposal package add up to a considerable investment. Don't be dismayed. You can do it if you follow these steps:

1. Obtain proposal application and the funding agency's most recent annual report as far in advance of the proposal deadline as possible. Perhaps you need to look at what emphasis the agency has for distributing funds and then work backward to develop a program or project that fits their goals. Read the annual report. Ask yourself:
   - Do we fit the goals and mission of this funding agency?
   - Can we adapt our proposed project to fit their criteria?
   - Is our proposal similar to the scope and goals of proposals this agency has awarded funds in the past?
   - Do we meet funding criteria?
   - Did they fund similar organizations or projects in our area?
   - Do we know anyone on their Board with whom we can discuss this proposal?
   - Can we discuss our proposal with an organization that has received funding from this group in the past?
   - Is it possible to collaborate with an organization that has received funding in the past to submit a cooperative project proposal?
   - Can we review our idea/proposal with a staff member of the funding agency before completing the formal application?
2. Read every word of the proposal application from the title through financial requirements to required signatures.
3. Make two copies of the blank application form and file one.
4. Use the second copy as a working copy.
5. Highlight the due date or postmark date required. If the proposal is not received on time, it will not be considered.
6. Review all financial data needed.
7. Check the number of copies you must submit along with other required information to avoid last-minute delays.
8. Keep copies of all materials you submit, including the completed application and financial and support information. When funded, keep in the project folder a copy of the check and award letter, all correspondence and interim and final reports. Also keep photos of the children participating in the project, copies of artwork, poetry, letters of support, news clippings and other documentation in this file.

Funding is a highly competitive business. When talking with other organizations about funding, be aware that groups with the most altruistic motives can get downright ugly when it comes to discussing funding sources with a potential rival.

City, county, state and federal funding applications are available for public review as a matter of public record. It is well worth the time to review proposals that were funded. Often there are evaluator notes on a proposal, which indicate the objectives of the review panel. Structure your proposal to fit the focus of the panel. It is interesting to see what projects are funded, their budgets and who wrote letters of support.

> **Make every effort to have representatives of funding organizations visit your site, especially when the children are in class. Seeing the children in a creative environment has an incredible impact on a visitor.**

We had a wonderful spokesman in Christopher. He lived next door to the Center and attended after-school art classes from first grade until high school. He was always ready to smile for a camera and give his candid opinions to anyone who asked. Chris was a treasure as a participant and as spokesman.

If you cannot arrange for a representative to visit your site, try to visit them at their office. Show them photos of the children involved in after-school activities. Take along a few samples of art projects and be prepared to relate stories about children who have grown through participating in after-school art programming.

Take Time to Evaluate Your Situation

Is the effort and cost of completing a proposal worth the amount of funding that it may generate? Is it worth $400 in time and materials to obtain $500 in funding? *Maybe.* It could open the door for future collaborations. Certain donors add prestige to a donor list.

Every funding proposal is a gamble. Even if you do not get the funding you request, the foundation may keep your proposal on file through the end of their fiscal year. If they have surplus funds to disperse at year-end, they may reconsider groups denied funds earlier in the year and issue you a surprise check.

Many funding sources do not fund a first-time request. They fund their "regulars." A review of your proposed project may pique their interest. Don't be surprised if they seek you out through an informal site visit or interview or the community grapevine. Invite them to visit your site even though they did not fund the project, just to see your program in action. When you submit a proposal in the next funding cycle, they will be more familiar with your organization. They may fund a small project or dollar request until a rapport is established with your organization.

Follow Application Directions Exactly

Do the instructions allow you to reproduce the form on your computer or must you use only the form provided? Do they restrict you to space provided on the form or can you attach pages? Even if not specified, type all information. If at all possible, use a computer or word processor with a good printer to complete the application and supplemental materials. If you must use a typewriter, use one that is self-correcting to create a neat final product without Whiteout blobs.

Submit only the materials requested with the application. Visuals such as photos of children working on a project, copies of children's artwork, and poetry or short stories may help evaluators understand your program or project idea. However, do not submit these with the application unless it is permissible to do so. Include these items with a follow-up letter inviting agency representatives to visit your program.

Do not send your application electronically without permission. Each application packet should be complete and professional in appearance. Funders may duplicate your proposal for members of the review panel. A bad original makes poor copies. No matter how worthy your proposal, if they can't read it, they will not consider it.

Save time. Plan ahead.

Plan ahead by creating stock descriptions of your organization to insert in the "describe your organization" section. Prepare typed two-inch, three-inch, five-inch and single-page descriptions in advance. These prepared paragraphs allow you a starting point from which to embark on narratives and present a consistent message for all proposals as well as public relations materials, appeal letters and other correspondence.

Put together a few good paragraphs that describe:
- **Who** your organization is
- **What** you do
- **Why** you do it
- **Where** you are located
- **How** you accomplish your goals

It is a challenge to get it all into a small space—those who do it well get the funding dollars.

Funding request: Why are you special?

Clearly and succinctly state why the organization should give you money, the amount of money you need, or any other request you have of them. They want to know:
- Why are you asking them to fund this project or organization?
- How do you reflect their goals or philosophy?
- What is in it for you?
- What is in it for them? Publicity? Goodwill?

- How will their investment bring the arts to children?
- How will you document that you achieved the stated goals?
- How much? Ask for a specified dollar amount or specific goods or services.

We wrote a grant proposal requesting 30 pair of white canvas tennis shoes in children's sizes from a local discount store. We received the shoes, which the children decorated with glitter and paint. The store received much publicity through donating the shoes and through newspaper photographs of the decorated shoes. The children and their families all appreciated the generosity of the store, generating goodwill for the business.

Administrative costs

It is important to understand that very few funding sources provide dollars for operating expenses. Therefore, it is critical that every funding proposal include a component to defray overhead. Factor in the cost of personnel, rent, utilities, telephone, office supplies, postage, consultants, insurance, rental of special tools, equipment, furniture, transportation, and computer and copy costs in your project budget. Be honest with the financial request and stay within the funding guidelines and criteria.

Qualified Personnel

"Qualified" does not necessarily mean persons must have advanced degrees. Your staff must have the training and experience (be it life, education or work) to get the job done at a fair rate of pay.

Success impresses reviewers. No one gives money to organizations with a poor financial track record. Those who show success and fiscal responsibility will get the dollars.

Resumés, newspaper interviews and letters of support from area business or professional people familiar with your staff and/or organization substantiate your credibility and ability to achieve the goals of your proposal. Keep an updated file of letters of support from area school principals, teachers, business organizations, social service agencies and neighbors, along with comments from children.

Materials

Be realistic about items needed to accomplish a project. Proposal reviewers can judge if funds requested suit the project and can realistically achieve the results predicted. They do not look kindly on a final report that says you did not accomplish your goals because you ran out of cash. If you are not sure what the project will cost, consult with them before you complete the proposal. Be honest and say that some financial factors are unknown. Keep the door open to come back for extra help if needed, or be prepared to develop ways to support the project should a shortfall occur. Some funding bodies may allow you an opportunity to extend your time or funding, but this is a rare situation.

Approach Several Potential Funding Sources

Receiving funds from several funders is not double dipping! Funding groups prefer to share the cost of a project. They feel more secure with a decision to fund knowing that another group also sees merit in the request. Unless a funder has exclusive rights to a project, they will be pleased that you are able to raise enough money to cover the project. Raising funds from several sources will help defray overhead expenses not always covered in specific project budgets.

Be honest with your financial statements, budgets and sources of funding.

Be sure that you list all funds received. If you lie or fail to disclose all in-kind support and cash received for the project, you may never get funding again. Do not jeopardize the reputation of your staff and organization by reporting inaccurate information.

Be prepared for a site visit by a representative of the funding agency before they consider your funding request. This visit may be by appointment or a surprise. Encourage visits while children are at your facility.

To determine a project start date and how to budget funds over the project period, ask the following:
- Does the funding agency board meet annually, quarterly or monthly to review requests?
- Is a letter of intent to apply for funds necessary?
- How far in advance of a board meeting is the letter of intent or proposal due?
- After review of the letter of intent, will a proposal be invited or automatically due by a certain date?
- When will they review the proposal?
- When will they make a decision?
- How and when will they inform us of their decision?
- If approved for funding, when can the project begin and when will funds be released?
- Will funds be dispersed in a lump sum at the beginning, end or specified times throughout the project period?
- Are funds received on a reimbursement basis?

Organization Financial Data

Balancing your financial records on a monthly basis is essential. It is often necessary to compare current year activity with the actual financial data for your most recently completed fiscal year in the following categories:

Revenue
- Earned income
- Foundation/corporate support

97

- Individual contributions
- Membership income
- Government funds
- United Way funds
- Special events/other fundraising income
- Matching grants
- In-kind donation of materials or services
- Investment income
- Projected budget for next year

Expenses
- Program
- Operating
- Administrative
- Development
- Other projected expenses for next year

Keep an updated list of corporate and private donors and amounts contributed annually as well as a list of confirmed donors to projects and the amounts pledged.

Maintain clean, up-to-date copies of the above information printed clearly on your letterhead and on plain paper to easily adapt it to various proposal formats.

Project Goals/Results/Evaluation

How well did you meet project goals within the financial projections? If you requested funds to have 50 people attend a seminar on multicultural arts education and only 45 attended, did you meet the goal? If you sought funds to have 200 children participate in a summer arts program and 250 participated, were you successful? If you received funds to coordinate four neighborhood groups into one art cooperative and only three groups decided to join, did you achieve your goal?

Document numbers and reactions. If your goal was 50 for the seminar and 45 attended, you were five persons short of the goal. However, more important is what the 45 who attended gained by their participation. What was the impact of the seminar? How did the speakers move the audience? Did you have the audience complete an exit survey evaluating their experience? Did 40 say it was great and why? Did 40 say it was a waste of time and why? Did you randomly call 25 percent of the participants one week after the seminar to see if they put into practice any of the principles they learned? Was there any press coverage of the event?

You need to compare goals with results in quantitative terms. Qualify those results with information gained from surveys, quotes, newspaper reviews, photographs, a videotape of the project and samples of artwork from the project.

If 250 children attended the summer art program, it was successful in terms of numbers. However, does that show a greater need than anticipated? Did you survey the families, teachers and the children to obtain feedback on the experience? Were there any language barriers or difficulties with communication? Did you have enough personnel to run the classes? Were there enough materials? Was there a competing program? Could you have made scheduling adjustments, added additional personnel or purchased more supplies to keep the children interested?

If only three of the four community groups who planned to collaborate on project decided to participate, does that make the project a failure? Maybe the fourth group dissolved. Perhaps funding was not really sufficient for all four groups to participate. The evaluation of the project should discuss the groups that participated and why the fourth did not. Most important is how effective the program was for the three groups that did participate.

Be prepared to make adaptations to the original project plan at any point in the process to insure success. If you perceive a problem with the project at any point, inform the funding organization as soon as possible. They may approve a delay of the project to resolve the problem or suggest that you proceed in another way. Keep the lines of communication open. Do not assume that you can make major changes from the presented proposal and no one will care. Communicate alternatives for changes in advance and obtain assurance that funding is still in place.

Keep accurate records of financial and other data associated with the project. Document as much of the project as possible by taking photos, video-taping activities and interviewing staff and participants throughout the process to get first-hand reactions. Encourage media representatives to visit and keep copies of reviews or news stories about the project. Be sure to credit all sources of funding and donors of in-kind services or goods when talking to the media about the project.

Submit your final report on time. Include all support material to document how the project met its goals as indicated above. Clearly list all financial data as requested by the funder. Be sure all required signatures are on the final report.

The children involved with the project might make a collage of photographs or prepare a booklet showing the group at work throughout the project to submit with the final report. Or they can make a small piece of art as a thank you for the funding organization.

Keep a copy of the final report in the project folder along with a copy of the original application, supporting information, interim reports and project documentation. Having this information available will facilitate preparation of future requests for this and other funding sources.

File the folder and then pour yourself a big glass of iced tea to celebrate your success.

A Review Checklist To Avoid Grantwriting Problems

1. Does project reflect current needs of the community?
   - Involve people from all aspects of community life when planning projects.
   - Try new and innovative ideas.

2. Is funding request appropriate for funding guidelines or review criteria?
   - Read entire grant guidelines or submission requirements before preparing application.
   - Understand program goals, priorities and evaluation criteria.
   - If unsure about meeting criteria, call the agency to discuss project/program with a grant officer.
   - Arrange for site visit if possible.

3. Is proposal difficult to read or understand?
   - Proofread proposal for spelling, grammar, math and typographical errors.
   - Have someone who did not prepare the application proofread it also.
   - A day or two after completing it, re-read the application before submitting it
   - Submit only a typed, reproducible application and attachments.
   - Avoid using jargon—use clear, concise wording.
   - Provide detail in financial and narrative sections to clearly describe project.
   - Don't repeat information in the narrative section. Choose words carefully to emphasize the most important aspects of the proposal.

4. Does proposal include only high-quality support materials?
   - Be sure printed support material is high-quality, relevant, and informational.
   - Submit only quality work samples via slides, videotape or photographs.
   - Submit only information that relates to the project or program.
   - Include support materials that are reproducible if needed by the review panel.

5. Is the application package complete?
   - Provide all required information and support materials as requested.
   - Follow directions exactly.
   - Adhere to format directions.
   - Double check that all materials are assembled before sending packet.

6. Is there technical assistance available to applicants?
   - If technical assistance is available, review proposal ideas before beginning the application
   - If possible, submit a draft application for staff review.
   - Request applications from previous years if available for review.

7. Are you clear on the application due date or postmark date?
   - The due date and postmark date are two different concepts. Be sure you know when the application must be received or postmarked so as to allow adequate time for mailing.
   - Consider sending the application by certified mail.
   - Always keep a complete copy of what was sent in your files.

8. Are you using the most recent application form?

9. Is application authorized by your governing board and signed by authorized official?
   - Obtain proper authority for proposal before submitting it to prospective funders.
   - Provide a copy of the application to the authorizing official or governing board.
   - Present all grant proposals to your governing board to include in your fundraising and programming plans.

10. What can you do after receiving a grant award?
    - Verify when interim and final reports are due.
    - Determine if funds will be distributed in advance or on a reimbursement basis.
    - Check details to conduct project in accordance with timelines and as proposed in the approved application.

c h a p t e r

14

Partnerships with Businesses

No matter where your program is located, small businesses or multinational corporations can become involved with after-school art programming. Business people know that an educated population provides a good source of employees. When an after-school program joins forces with local businesses, young people benefit and area businesses have an opportunity to develop good public relations.

Why should businesses get involved?

Most businesses support education. Educated young people become good employees, good neighbors and good consumers. A company involved in programs such as after-school art programs becomes a significant player in helping to improve the standards of the community by reaching our most precious resource—children. Youngsters involved in positive after-school activities are less likely to get in trouble. They are less likely to become involved with underage drinking, drug use, gang affiliation, shoplifting and other petty or major crime.

How do you start a partnership?

1. Know what you expect from a partnership. How will helping your program benefit the firm and the community? When approaching the business community, focus on how partnering with your after-school art program will benefit them.
2. Determine which business to approach based on its proximity to your site, the products or services it offers and perhaps whether it employs the parents of children who would attend your program,
3. Arrange to meet with a company decision-maker: President, Marketing Director, Human Resource representative or Branch Manager. Be willing to cooperate with any offer of support and then build on positive interactions.
4. If you are not successful with a business, analyze why they chose not to help, adjust your approach and then move on to another. If appropriate, ask why they were unable to help you at this time.

How can businesses help your program?

The most obvious way for a business to support art after school programs is through a cash contribution. Some firms have foundations through which they funnel charitable contributions. Find out about the application process and funding parameters before you submit an application for consideration. The foundation board will review your application to see if you meet their criteria. You may get what you asked for, a smaller amount, or nothing. The thin envelope usually is bad news. The thicker reply envelope often means there are additional forms to fill out before you receive a dollar award.

Cash is great, but businesses also can help by donating employee time or materials as in-kind donations, such as:

- Flex-time for employees to mentor, teach, do minor repairs and offer clerical or computer skills
- Metal or plastic pieces from the manufacturing process to use in collages, jewelry or sculpture pieces
- Paper for drawing
- Chairs, tables, desks, computers, copiers and other office equipment left over after upgrading equipment or remodeling offices
- Old wallpaper books from a paint or wallpaper store to make collages, greeting cards or clothing for paper dolls
- Paint to decorate and brighten studio space
- Food for children's snacks
- Fabric for quilts, costumes or drop cloths
- Topsoil for a garden
- Wood chips for a play lot

In-kind donations are materials or goods that a business donates instead of cash. Count these goods or services as "in-kind" income on your financial statements. Use in-kind donations to supplement a cash match. A donor may promise to give you $2,000 if you raise $2,000 in cash or obtain goods or services equivalent to $2,000. You may raise $500 in cash and then $1,500 of in-kind (donated) goods and services. Place a reasonable value on items or time donated when accounting for them.

Useful in-kind donations we have received or that we suggest:

- Rolls of telephone wire from a telephone company. Use the inner brightly colored wires to make jewelry, cover picture frames or build sculpture pieces.
- Energy efficient ceiling lights from the electric company for the gallery and classroom areas.
- A copy machine and a computer such as those donated by Miller Brewing Company when they upgraded their office equipment.
- Use of their photography lab for a photography project, a helpful gift to us from a local college.

• Used folding chairs such as those we received from a manufacturing company. Artists and children painted the chairs in a variety of motifs from fine art representations to pop art. The chairs were painted so cleverly that they were auctioned at a fundraising event.

There are no limits. Research what area companies manufacture or process. How can you turn their leftovers or discards into a resource for your program? How can you return their generosity?

Always personally and publicly acknowledge support you receive from area businesses. Business people know the power of advertising and the importance of a positive public image. When you recognize a business contribution through a news release or newsletter article, the public sees that the business is community-minded and that your program must be worthwhile to receive such support.

Mr. P's Tire Store

Mr. P. has a chain of used-tire stores that would not win beautification awards. The director knew a sculptor willing to work with ten eleven-year-olds on a project. She contacted Larry, the manager of the tire store down the street, to see if he had tires we could use for the sculpture project. He said sure, about 150 tires.

He agreed to have the artist and children paint tires and create a sculpture in his store lot. For two weeks the artist and the ten children painted tires in the store's side lot on a busy street. They constructed a 12-foot man made of tires they painted with bright colors and designs. Mr. P's employees cheered the young artists along. The employees became friends with the kids as they

worked and took pride in their tire man sculpture that adds to the ambiance of the neighborhood.

The artists, children and employees all had fun with this project. They felt comfortable working together, showing off and bantering with neighbors as they passed by. The children felt welcome at Mr. P's to chat with the employees and Larry. Both sides became friendly neighbors. Children who worked on the project are still proud of what they did when they see "their" tire man.

Mr. P. received an incredible amount of positive feedback from area residents who saw the kids working on the sculpture and the whimsical finished product.

About this time we began training a team of teenagers to do murals on area buildings. Mr. P. agreed to have the teenagers paint his storefront with a bright mural design. The storefront had unusual siding of wood and lathe that was worn and tagged with graffiti. We arranged for two artists to work with a group of kids to design and paint a mural on the storefront.

Passersby frequently called to the children and artists to tell them what a great job they were doing. People driving by would honk their car horns and give the thumbs up sign. Mr. P. paid for the paint and a stipend for the artists and the children. In return, he received a freshly painted storefront that is distinctive and attractive. The finished product is delightful.

One major plus to having area kids work on neighborhood projects is that pieces are rarely tagged with graffiti or damaged. The kids who work on the art would not damage their own work, nor would their friends or relatives. A code of respect develops over murals.

The Pepto Bismol Car

Every community has its share of abandoned used cars. We partnered with an agency that trains low-income youth to be auto mechanics and learn to do body work on old cars. The agency donated two car bodies—an old Volkswagen and a subcompact car to use as sculpture pieces for a business district block party. The goal of the project was to make the kids aware of the advertising that surrounds us and how firms attract attention to their businesses.

The city arts board provided a grant to cover this project. Artist Mark Lawson spent several weeks during the summer working with kids to transform the two beat-up, rusting car bodies into attention-getting, marketing tools for area businesses. The kids looked at the cars and made several sketches of ideas.

They agreed to paint the Volkswagen a nice bright pink, putting a pig snout on the front and a little piggy tail on the back. They created a slot on the top and poised a large wooden coin half way through the slot to transform it into a large pink piggy bank! Adults who saw the car thought it to be the exact replica of Pepto Bismol pink.

The other car had a longer rounded body. The kids decided to paint it battleship gray. They painted porthole windows around the sides and converted it into a submarine, complete with a periscope on the roof.

Because the cars were just shells, it was easy to transport them for display at a merchant block party three miles away. The boys had a delightful time helping move the cars in the artist's pickup truck. They were full of excitement from the moment they realized they would be working on "real" cars and using real power tools. They were amazed to see their cars on display for the public. The cars were a delightful attraction at the festival. After the block party, two businesses used the submarine and pink piggy bank cars as signage.

Local newspapers ran photos of the cars at the block party. Press coverage reinforced the benefits of an after-school art program by showcasing successful projects. Include copies of these types of newspaper photos and articles with final reports to funding agencies to document the project and use of funds.

Collaboration with businesses produces friendly interaction among people who might otherwise not get to know one another. Through our collaborations, local business people became familiar with the kids and they greeted each other on the street. This rapport is what keeps a community strong and builds future ties. When these kids are old enough for part-time or full-time employment, the business people who met them through art after school programming are more likely to hire them because of this networking opportunity.

"We enjoy seeing the children come out of the art center taking their projects home. They are always smiling. Other times we see them, they don't look very happy."

Employee, car shop across the street

chapter 15

Publicity and Public Relations

A solid publicity and public relations plan is necessary from the moment you begin organizing your after-school art program. Publicity is necessary to inform and educate children, parents, educators, area residents, businesses and potential donors about your program.

Do not limit publicity just to print and broadcast. View all correspondence, meetings and speaking engagements as opportunities to spread the word about the philosophy, goals and merits of your program.

As you embark upon a publicity campaign, keep in mind that your overall goals are to:
- Encourage children to attend after-school and summer classes
- Inform the community about the merits of the program
- Attract volunteers
- Encourage donations of money, goods and services
- Document projects for donors
- Publicly acknowledge donors
- Report successful activities of the children

Be Aware of Copyright Laws

When you take photographs of children or anyone associated with your program, document whenever possible:
- The name of each person in the photograph
- Date and place of the activity
- Name of funding organization (if any) associated with the activity
- Permission allowing you to photograph the person(s). The release should also grant unrestricted reproduction of the photograph for publicity or other uses.
- Permission from the artist to reproduce photographs of their work for publicity purposes.

When a publication prints a story or photograph about an activity that you might want to reproduce in a newsletter or other format, contact the publication for permission to reproduce the article. You may have to pay a fee, but doing so shortly after publication will save a lot of time and frustration if you choose to reproduce the article later. Always get permission in writing.

For photographs, you will need permission from the publication as well as the photographer to reproduce the photograph. Fees and permission procedures vary widely. Even though a source gives you verbal consent, obtain permission in writing or follow up with a letter to the publication/photographer verifying the conversation you had with them and on what date they gave you permission to reproduce the requested item.

Develop a Logo for Your Program

Give your program a specific identity by developing a logo or letterhead design for stationery and envelopes. Your logo is your identity mark for correspondence, program fliers and signage.

Select clip art or design a simple graphic that copies well. Check with local graphic design firms, advertising agencies, art education departments or artist groups for someone to create a design for you *pro bono* (free). Ask area printers to print your letterhead and envelopes at a reduced or non-profit rate. Approach businesses or civic groups to underwrite printing costs.

Art After School Program Brochure

One of the basic elements in your publicity arsenal is an attractive, colorful brochure describing your program.

Brochures can be computer-designed and duplicated on brightly colored paper inexpensively. If no one on your staff is proficient in computer design, perhaps an intern or a member of your board will be able to help you come up with an attractive brochure.

As your program develops, update the brochure to include photos of children working on projects. You do not have to spend a lot of money to develop a promotional piece with impact.

Develop several boilerplate paragraphs and letters that describe your program. Prepare a concise paragraph of three or four sentences, a two-paragraph, and a one-page description. Both your long and short formats should explain:
- The Art After School program
- Organization mission statement
- Participants and staffing
- Location
- Reason for being established
- Organization and funding

Prepared written descriptions save time when you need to describe the program quickly. You need information in various lengths to submit to media, organizations, funding groups and sources for grants. Take time to prepare descriptions so your message is clear, accurate and consistent. You can always change or expand general descriptions as needed. With these basics in hand, you can now ratchet up your publicity campaign.

Publicity Calendar

Prepare a publicity calendar that lists all print and broadcast media in your area, as well as church bulletins, group newsletters and other information outlets to disseminate information about your program. Contact your local Chamber of Commerce or Press Club to see if they print a local media guide.

Indicate for each newspaper, magazine, television or radio station the name(s) of the person(s) to direct press releases to, including the address, telephone number, date required and format requested. Some organizations will accept press releases electronically; others will not.

Update this list regularly. Make an effort to meet the people you are sending press releases to or speaking to on the telephone about your program events. The personal touch allows you to understand their needs and gives them a better idea about you and your program.

Sometimes we dashed out weekly press releases at the last minute. To save time and money, Administrator Marlene Jaglinski and college interns would stuff freshly printed press releases into pre-addressed envelopes and then dash around town delivering them. Marlene would drive and the intern would hop out of the car at each media stop to hand deliver the "hot off the copier" latest information.

We made the job fun by playing loud jazzy music and picking up lunch at a new spot after each run. We do not advocate this as a regular method of disseminating your information. Planning ahead and getting the message out well in advance of the activity being publicized is the rule-of-thumb to follow with the media.

Mass Media

Assess the media available in your community to disseminate information about your program. Besides major newspapers and radio and television stations, submit press releases to special-interest groups through newsletters distributed by churches, senior citizen, 4-H clubs, colleges, civic groups and social service agencies such as Head Start centers. Submit information to businesses for their employee newsletters.

Do not overlook foreign language newspapers or broadcast stations. Send your copy in English unless you are fluent in their language. Their staff will translate your information or print or read it in English.

Treat your publicity as news, but do not limit yourself to the news section of newspapers or broadcast media. Send your press releases to the attention of editors and reporters who cover the arts, education, ethnic happenings, social news and business.

Look for angles that can give your story a different spin or outlet.

News releases to the various sections should emphasize a special aspect of the project or the person (artist) that makes it newsworthy or interesting.

- An artist in residence can be featured in local news, education pages or art news.
- A collaboration with a local business can be featured in news, art, business or education sections of a newspaper or magazine.
- An art project spotlighting an ethnic group or tradition is appropriate for news, community features, education or art.
- Special events and fundraising parties should be announced in advance of the event and later reported on in the social pages.

Send along a quality photograph (with permission to reproduce it). Encourage newspapers to photograph the children and projects in action. Invite local television and radio stations to cover the activity for a positive feature during the nightly newscast.

Encourage reporters to visit your center and interview the children. Prepare the children by letting them know that someone from the press might visit. Help them practice answering questions about their art and the program so they feel comfortable talking about themselves and the Art After School program with reporters and other visitors to your program.

Prepare news releases that rely on basic journalism guideposts to answer the questions: **Who? What? When? Why? Where? How?**

Children are Key

Children are key to any after-school art education program. No matter what parents, teachers or the community may think about your program, it is the children who must be persuaded to attend classes. Fliers about your program should be bright and inviting. Each flier should be written in English and any other language necessary to reach the people in your neighborhood.

Distribute new fliers each month listing class times and the address and telephone number of the center. Design fliers to briefly describe class projects and special events featured that month. Distribute fliers directly to children through schools and to parents through PTA groups. Post fliers at Head Start locations, in area coin laundries, libraries, playgrounds, parks, recreation programs, food stores, banks, barber shops, doctor and dentist offices and public health clinics. They can be inserted into church bulletins and distributed at food programs and social service sites.

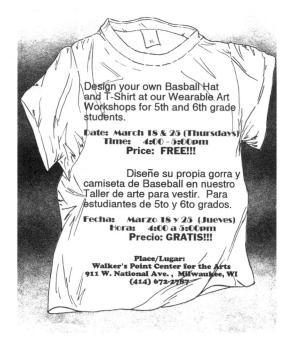

Winter Art Fun!

Join the Fun in January!

Free After-School Art Classes for Children in grades 2-8.

In January we will be making Silly Snakes, Mexican Yarn Paintings, miniature Costa Rican Ox Carts, and Animalitos.

Wednesdays   3:00-4:30

Thursdays   4:30-5:30

For more information call Debbie at 672-2787.

****

Clases de Arte-Despres de la Escuela-Gratis para nino y ninas de grades 2-8.

Miercoles   3:00-4:30

Jueves   4:30-5:30

WALKER'S POINT CENTER FOR THE ARTS
911 West National Avenue
672-2787

Show Sample Projects

Fliers tell your story, but sample projects are more convincing than words for children, parents and teachers. Make up a few samples of upcoming class projects to display at your center, in school lobbies, libraries, churches, banks, restaurants, barber shops, coin laundries and sites where you distribute fliers. Not every place will be suitable to display the project or willing to do so. Determine which is more effective for fliers and which is better for displays or storyboards.

Create a storyboard of photos showing children working on projects, wearing t-shirts, hats or other clothing they decorated, or participating in a performance. Children who see other children having fun will be encouraged to join in. Display the boards in local businesses on a rotating basis. Update the boards regularly.

If you have window space or a storefront, display projects there as well. Displaying class projects and photo storyboards of the children at work on projects is a great way for the children to show parents and friends what they do in class. The community will enjoy the displays and may encourage someone to volunteer their time or donate materials to your program. It is fun to see little Maria or Danny pointing to their picture and saying, "That's me. Look what I did!"

The fliers, projects and photograph displays remind the entire community about your program and the great opportunity it provides for the children. Community residents look forward to seeing the changing displays and photos.

Samples give a visual imprint of the activities. Samples also foster creativity, teach certain life skills, illustrate how to integrate art and academics, and instill the personal pleasure and satisfaction achieved through art.

Take along sample projects when you meet with any community group or media representatives. If possible, bring the artist who will be working with the children to do a small project with the group and explain the dynamics of the art.

A well-designed publicity plan will encourage people to volunteer their time or services and donate supplies or money because they see what a fun, educational and positive activity art after-school can be. They will want to be a part of it.

Publicity Costs

Press releases are your most cost-effective way to disseminate information about your program to the general public. Costs include postage, paper, envelopes and staff time to write, photocopy, deliver or mail the release.

Weekly or monthly mailings to the free community calendar sections of local publications and broadcast media are a consistent way to promote your program or needs to the public. To cut costs, ask a volunteer or intern to do this function on a weekly or monthly basis. Consider the cost and effectiveness of faxing or using e-mail to send your press releases if you have the technology available.

Monthly fliers distributed through a variety of outlets can be expensive if you use fancy or bright paper. But it is worth the added cost to encourage children to attend your after-school arts program. Draw fliers by hand or create them on a computer. A school may let you use a computer to create the fliers once a month. You also might be able to recruit a college intern or volunteer to do the fliers on a home or school computer.

Someone fluent in the written and oral aspects of the language should do translations from English to other languages. A language teacher or advanced student can help do this.

Paper costs can be reduced if you buy paper in bulk. Seek donations from businesses or paper left over from jobs run by area printers or advertising firms. Use plain white paper to cut costs. Embellish or highlight copies used as posters to attract attention when posted.

Photographing children and projects can get expensive due to the cost of cameras, film, video equipment and film processing. Check with local high schools and colleges for photography, film and video classes or clubs. Encourage instructors to send students to photograph children and projects at least once per semester. This collaboration provides an interesting setting where the photography students can practice, and in return you get a photo essay or video of children and projects. You save the cost of film, equipment and processing, but may have to pay for reprints of photos or copies of the video.

Photos are invaluable to send in publicity packages, letters to funding sources, businesses and thank you notes. The children enjoy seeing photos or videotape of themselves and their class working on a project in the media. Have photography consent forms and artwork waiver forms (samples at the end of this chapter) signed by the parent or guardian of each child in your program.

Don't Forget the Budget

Budgeting for publicity is essential. Every program and project budget must include a publicity allowance. You cannot conduct classes or do a project without letting children know about it. Some projects will require that the final exhibit or performance be open to the public. Be sure to include the costs of invitations and publicity in the project budget. Film and film processing expenses are components of the publicity budget.

Publicity costs include:
- Staff time to prepare publicity
- Stationery and envelopes
- Printing
- Photocopies
- Postage, fax or e-mail
- Photographic equipment, film, prints, videos
- Sample projects

Be realistic. Remember to tally time and materials donated as in-kind. Account for these services and goods as matching dollars in grant budgets where a dollar match is required. List in-kind goods and services on your income statement and program budget.

After-School Art Program Newsletter

Distribute a quarterly newsletter to donors, media personnel, members and other individuals who contribute to or support your program. The newsletter can be a one- or two-page summary concerning events, participating artists and other highlights of the quarter. Include a color photo page showing the children and artists at work together.

A newsletter informs donors as to activities and shows them how their money is being used. It is a nice way to stay in touch without asking for money and shows how their contributions are having a positive impact on children. Donors appreciate the updates throughout the year. It is easier to ask them to contribute when you have kept in touch.

List all donors to a particular project or all your donors on any program you print for an open house, performance or exhibit. Again, do not forget those who gave cash, in-kind donors and volunteers.

Always list donors per their request. Do not list Mrs. Helen Schwartz if it should be the Michael and Helen Schwartz Family Foundation. DETAILS COUNT!

Say "Thank you."

Your newsletter should always thank donors for making your program possible. It is also important to thank media personnel who help you by printing or broadcasting your information. Thank the person who let you put fliers at the grocery store or the barber who puts fliers in his shop window. Say thank you and write thank you notes. Include a picture of the children at work on a project.

Have the children make little thank you projects periodically to give to those who help with publicity, to your major donors and to special volunteers. Art created by the children such as a decorated picture frame with a photo of them at work or a card they made as a thank you is very effective. The gift that the children create not only conveys their appreciation, but helps the children become aware of people in the community who help make the program a reality for them. Everyone wants to be appreciated.

Greeting card created by Hands On student

Electronic Communication

On-site access to a computer system with fax and e-mail capabilities is truly a cost-effective time saver for communication. If you can fax or e-mail your publicity, do so. You should also mail a copy of your press release, particularly when sending out material well in advance of an event. A hard copy also helps ensure that the information is directed to the right person. Send a hard copy when including a photo or visual that will not transmit well electronically.

Target Your Community

Each community is unique. Try new ways to inform your neighborhood about your programming. Ideas to try:
- Submit press releases to area businesses for their internal employee newsletters—a great way to recruit volunteers or request donations of supplies
- Stuff fliers in neighborhood "shopper" newspapers
- Create small table cards for area restaurants that describe your program and list public events
- Offer to speak about Art After School on local talk shows
- Ask a local television station to interview children who participate, and show the children at work on projects
- Have students create sculpture pieces for a company picnic/party
- Have students make posters to advertise events for civic groups
- Ask area store and restaurant owners to put donation boxes at their cashier stations for people to drop their spare change. Be sure to have a system for collecting the money periodically. Thank participating businesses by giving them a special thank you item suggested above.

Here are sample photography consent and artwork waiver forms. Check with your legal advisor to adjust the wording to meet the needs of your organization. It is most efficient to include the consent language for the photography and artwork waivers on the registration form that the parents/guardians complete for each child attending your program.

Photography Consent Form

Name of Your Organization

I, _____, (circle one) consent/do not consent to be photographed, videotaped, audio-taped and/or interviewed by the news media while participating in *Your Program Name*. I agree to hold harmless and release the *Your Program Name*, its members, officials, agents and employees from and against all claims, demands, actions, complaints, suits or other forms of liability that shall arise out of, or by reason of, or be caused by the use of my image on television, radio, motion pictures or in the print media.

I agree that no monies or other consideration in any form including reimbursement for expenses incurred by me will come due to me, my heir, agents or assigns at any time because of my participation in any of the above activities.

Signed_____ Date_____
(Parent or guardian if above is under 18 years old)

Print Name_____

Artwork Waiver Statement

I,_____, agree that any artwork that I produce in whole or in part as a participant in *Your Program Name*, including but not limited to any and all paintings, sculptures, photographs, videotapes, architectural drawings or models, literary works, musical compositions or recordings are all and shall remain the property of *Your Program Name* and I have no proprietary interest in said artwork.

Signed_____ Date_____
(Parent or guardian if above is under 18 years old)

Print Name_____

chapter 16

Art After School Goals and Philosophy: Encourage Creativity in Children

All the facets of after-school art programming come together to make a unique educational, cultural and social contribution to a neighborhood through art. By putting into action the principles discussed earlier in the book, you will stir the imaginations of children, and they will learn.

Creative thinking enhances fundamentals learned in school while providing children an opportunity to express themselves as unique individuals with their own personal vision.

As self-esteem grows through increased creative empowerment, so does motivation for personal and external exploration. Stimulating the imagination through making art arouses several dimensions of learning. The arts inspire creative thinking when children participate in and view art, concerts and plays and when they interact with artists.

Jane Brite, the original Director of Walker's Point Center for the Arts, was a student at Crow Island, a John Dewey school in Winnetka, Illinois. Dewey was an American philosopher and educator whose writings had a profound influence on education in the United States. He was America's most famous exponent of pragmatic education, celebrating the traditional values of democracy, the efficacy of reason, and universal education that focused on learning by doing. This concept differed from the rote learning and dogmatic instruction techniques practiced in his day.

Dewey reasoned that art is not only what we see in museums or classical structures such as the Parthenon in Greece. Movies, jazz and comic strips are all art forms we take for granted, but they are often not considered art. However, we enjoy these art forms as they relate to our humanness.

John Dewey in his book, *Art as Experience*, demonstrates that the existence of art is concrete proof that man uses the materials and energies of nature to expand his own life through use of his intelligence and senses. Dewey contends that man consciously chooses to vary the arts in many ways, based upon his needs and impulses. Dewey holds that art is a conscious idea that stands as the greatest intellectual achievement in the history of humanity.

Brite feels the after-school art model developed from her experience in the Crow Island free-thinking and hands-on learning environment. Studies show that intelligence is manifested in different ways in different individuals—some are more intellectually oriented, others more creatively oriented.

Howard Gardner, co-director of Project Zero at the Harvard Graduate School of Education and adjunct Professor of Neurology at Boston University's School of Medicine, offers alternative visions of intelligence: "Learning is a pluralistic view of mind, recognizing many different and discrete facets of cognition, acknowledging that people have different cognitive strengths and contrasting cognitive styles." According to Gardner, who has written several books on the subject of intelligence and learning, "We are all so different largely because we all have different combinations of intelligence."

From the beginning, it was our policy at the Center to treat each child with non-judgmental enthusiasm, whether they caught on quickly or not, if they seemed particularly skillful or imaginative or not. We did not compare projects to each other and continually encouraged each child. Language difficulties, social experiences and financial situations put many of the children at a disadvantage when it came to understanding certain concepts presented in school and everyday life. However when making art they could transcend language and social barriers and communicate through their work. When given the same materials to work with, the playing field was leveled so each child to create as he or she wished to do.

Creative people tend to have many different responses to situations; some are idiosyncratic and possibly unique. Creativity energizes a person to think freely and welcome opportunities for innovative responses and problem solving.

Art is seeing, feeling and thinking about the world and communicating our feelings and thoughts to express what is inside us—love, anger, frustration or happiness.

Chris Vega, as a high school junior, reminisced about his experiences in the Hands On, after-school art program from first through eighth grade. He felt that interaction with the Center staff and artists and working on a wide array of art through the years made him feel good about himself. He grew secure in his ideas and feelings, which enabled him to retain his individualism and not succumb to negative peer pressure. Chris believed his positive experiences reinforced his self-image, making him proud of personal choices, such as being a vegetarian, doing art and playing sports for fun.

An after-school art program can encourage children to be comfortable with their individuality. They can look at themselves and others with fresh eyes and minds. They are encouraged to learn about and respect differences. They learn not to let financial constraints curb their abilities to create art.

Through the arts, children learn to trust their instincts and vision. In a non-judgemental setting, art gives them the freedom to re-shape what they see until it expresses their intent or reaction. Positive reinforcement lavished sincerely allows children to experience both joy from what they make and the process and freedom of creativity. It may give them a reason to be.

Many teenagers said they enjoyed classes and participating in projects because it gave them a reason to get out of bed and a place to be besides the street corner. But they know that some of their decisions to submit to peer pressures are wrong. They don't always know how to make things better for themselves or what alternatives they have. While working productively and learning, young people get to know responsible adults whom they can talk to. The instructors may serve as mentors who casually, as conversations come up, discuss problems, hopes or dilemmas. This one aspect alone can make a significant difference in the life of a child or teenager and is well worth every dollar put into after-school programs.

"You know that you must be doing something right when the kids keep coming back to classes. They don't have to be there. This is their free time. It is a chance for them to create their own vision—a chance to push their creativity."

Mark Lawson
Artist

119

Use the arts to encourage. . .

- An atmosphere of trust and a spirit of fun
- Openness to dream and question
- Simple expectations, praise and cooperation
- Opportunities to change minds and go in new directions
- A stimulating, even entertaining atmosphere
- A sense of pleasure in one's own creativity
- Win-win situations for children
- Acceptance of mistakes. They are ways to explore and exploration is never a waste of time
- Constructive support, not criticism
- An atmosphere with a few simple rules

The Art After School model stresses using artists to teach classes whenever possible because artists offer a delightful openness and spontaneity. Usually they are unencumbered by the structure and control of traditional school settings. Art as a shared activity between child and artist allows for dialogue that goes beyond a particular activity or project. Children learn about the artist as a person with different experiences and visions. The artist learns about each child and who he or she is based upon individual lives and dreams.

"I brought a big circular fish net which spread to 15' in diameter. We all held on to the edges of the net and in unison lifted and then dropped it to the cement floor. We imagined what fish we might catch together—we drew with colored chalk the fish we imagined on the floor. The room became a gigantic aquarium. We told fishing stories. We named the fish—using the many native languages of the children participating. It was an adventure. Cooperative spirit reigned but originality and individualities were expressed in a spirit of fun and sharing. I still think about the magical day we spent together at Walker's Point. The next day I saw a photograph of our art on the front page of the morning newspaper. Our discovery of and affirmation of life—creatively expressed—was NEWS!"

Sheila Hicks
International Fiber Artist

Whoever conducts classes must be a leader, not a master. The teacher/artist serves as a guide, someone to encourage and prompt others. Making and observing art is a deep and harmonizing experience. It can set standards for each of us, enhance the life of each child at a particular time, and have lifelong influences. Artists as teachers provide invaluable models for students through their passion and perspective as strong creative beings and can help turn children into excited, inventive individuals.

Presenting children with samples of the activity to take place at each class session is very important. Samples show them what they can do and give them a place from which to go forward. Some children start out copying the sample. However, when they learn to use what they see as an inspiration, they will make their own art based on who they are at the moment and what they want their work to be.

Individualism is important, yet children need to learn to work together in small or large groups. Give children ownership in the program by including them from idea to completion. They learn to experiment and stick with a project, even when it becomes difficult to achieve the final goal. Through group dynamics we expand upon each other's ideas, choose projects of interest to all and each feel a part of the outcome.

Urban Garden Project

An urban garden project is an excellent example of how to implement Art After School goals and philosophies because it can:

- Give young people opportunities to interact on a one-to-one basis with gardeners, architects, artists and volunteers
- Afford opportunity for creative expression and pleasure
- Help children build pride in their accomplishments when visitors compliment them on the beautiful garden they helped create
- Reinforce the academic principles of science, math and design
- Develop awareness of art and the environment
- Force children to use problem-solving strategies to overcome financial, design and other obstacles
- Introduce them to a variety of career possibilities from architecture to horticulture that they might not otherwise have thought about

The Center did a mailing to area garden clubs asking them to help support renovating a debris-strewn, back-lot parking area into an urban garden. Over $600 in donations was received for the project. Gigi Schroeder, an intern from the University of Wisconsin–Milwaukee (UWM), coordinated the project. UWM school of architecture professor Douglas Rhyn arranged for a landscape architecture student to develop design ideas based upon the following considerations:

- Children must be able to help create the space.
- The finished space must be user-friendly, a place for children to do their art and enjoy seclusion away from the bustling city beyond the fence.
- The finished space must be multi-purpose to use for receptions, fundraising events and additional gallery space for exhibiting art.
- The children must be able to plant and help maintain the space.

Bill O'Dell, a retired engineer, built the fence with the help of several children. They built flower boxes along the fence with a wide, low ledge to serve as a retaining wall and garden seating along the perimeter of the garden. Margarete Harvey, a local landscape architect, suggested plants based on sunny

and shady areas and ease of maintenance. Individuals donated seeds and plants. The garden grew each season with a variety of colors, textures and sights as the children and artists added new dimensions to the space with injections of vitality and whimsical sculptures.

Children were instrumental in the project, discussing plans, pulling weeds and cleaning the lot before construction. Several projects centered on how plants grow, planting seeds and decorating containers. The children learned patience while waiting for their seeds to germinate and grow into flower and vegetable seedlings to plant outdoors. The children especially liked seeing the bean plants grow up the fence and plucking the fresh beans for a snack. They enjoyed watching little pumpkin seeds become large orange orbs to carve and decorate. They did not enjoy weeding the garden on hot afternoons, watering the plants every day or cleaning debris from the space. However, they learned that some unpleasant tasks are necessary to have a space of beauty and pleasure.

Art projects in the garden included sketching plants, doing leaf rubbings and creating sculptures for the space. The garden is a perfect place for teachers and artists to read to the children and share their daily snack.

The children were encouraged to enjoy the building process and outcome of their urban garden experience. They applied scientific and mathematical concepts to complete the project. They learned to feel comfortable communicating their needs and ideas to a variety of people while becoming aware of occupations such as architecture and horticulture. They learned it is important to stay with and complete long-and short-term projects and improvise to find creative solutions to problems as they arose. They enjoyed using hand and power tools with adult supervision

We can enhance our eyes, ears and intuition as we learn about and participate in the arts. We become more aware of the people and things that surround us. We hear sounds and see sights from new perspectives that broaden our view of humanity and culture. Children can learn that art is a part of everyday life. Art crosses social barriers because the impulse for creativity is within everyone, no matter what his or her circumstances. Art shows us how we are each different and yet the same. Art-making reinforces children's notions of themselves as unique individuals who are a part of a community.

> "I think about children and teaching as using the mind, the hands, and the heart. My experience teaching at Walker's Point Center for the Arts incorporated this attitude. The children became participants in the community through some of our projects. I remember doing masks and working together in the presence of television cameras—many of the children found a few minutes of fame on television. We worked on murals—everyone having a role, everyone working together. We made gifts for Mother's Day. But more than what we produced as art was what we gave to one another. I became a part of their neighborhood and they became a part of my heart."
>
> Barbara Kohl-Spiro
> Artist/Teacher

Chris attended the after-school art program for several years. He has made art a part of his everyday life. He has taken to decorating his small front yard and porch for every holiday as well as planting flowers to enliven his home. Chris lives with his mother and aunt. He comments that they didn't always understand the creations he made in the after-school art classes, but they realized that he really enjoyed spending time at the Center—doing the artwork and meeting interesting people.

Realizing that you can create and that in the arts there is not a right or wrong way—only your way—is a cleansing experience. You become free to do, say, sing or dance in your own way. Not everyone will enjoy or understand what you do or why you do it, but it is important and enjoyable to you. You created it. You figured out how to do it. You chose the colors or format. It makes a statement: Creativity is in each of us—go for it!

Harvard professor Howard Gardner in his 1993 book, Multiple Intelligences, *emphasizes the importance of using projects to demonstrate and teach. "The course of project construction gives rise to opportunities for new understanding. Projects provide an opportunity for students to marshal previously mastered concepts and skills in the service of a new goal or enterprise. The knowledge of how to draw on such earlier forms of representation or understanding to meet a new challenge is a vital acquisition. Planning the project, taking stock along the way, rehearsing it, assembling it in at least tentative final form, answering questions about it, and viewing the tape critically should all help to enhance the student's understanding of the topic of the project, as well as their own contributions to it realized."*

Gardner, Howard (1993) Multiple Intelligences. New York; Harper Collins Publishers, Inc. p.12

Gardner, Howard (1993) Multiple Intelligences. New York; Harper Collins Publishers, Inc. p.6

Gardner, Howard (1993) Multiple Intelligences. New York; Harper Collins Publishers, Inc. p.117

How the Hands On, Art After School Program Began

Walker's Point was one of the three original settlements that grew to become the City of Milwaukee. Its early inhabitants were Irish, Polish and German immigrants. Today it is predominantly Hispanic, some African-American, third-and fourth-generation Polish and some Asian-American. Economically the neighborhood spans middle-class to poverty-level households.

The Walker's Point area is gaining new life through a resurgence of businesses taking advantage of low rents. Abandoned factories are being rehabbed into small manufacturing or service firms. People are buying small homes to rehabilitate with low-interest loans.

This neighborhood is "the" place to go for Mexican food. Many artists live or have studio space in the area. The Milwaukee Ballet studio is located in what once was a Schlitz Beer Palm Garden. Non-profit organizations offer training programs to low-income residents. The area is a hub for cultural and educational activities that target the area's Hispanic population.

Despite the revitalization of the area, there is a high crime rate and a proliferation of graffiti, gangs and drugs.

Walker's Point Center for the Arts (WPCA) developed in a two-story corner building that had been, among other things, a pharmacy and rooming house. WPCA was the idea of a businesswoman with a love of the arts and a vision of this neighborhood as one that would develop into an avant-garde mix of new offerings.

After six months of struggling with finances and building inspectors the Center opened in September of 1987 with a show spotlighting the works of painter Dennis Nectival and photographer Irene Adamcyk, and a musical performance by Brian Ritchie of the Violent Femmes.

At the suggestion of *Milwaukee Journal* art critic James Auer, the WPCA Board appointed Jane Brite Director/Curator in May of 1987. Valerie Christell was hired as Administrator.

From the start, the Center strove to avoid gentrification by involving the neighborhood in activities whenever possible. The goal was to be an integral part of the neighborhood. A concerted effort was made to patronize area businesses, including the corner grocery store, restaurants and a local bank.

In early 1988, WPCA contracted with Sherry Healy, a creator of handmade paper from Michigan, to do handmade paper sculptures. Since the artist was willing to work with children, Center staff contacted Robert Koeper, principal of Vieau Elementary School, located across the street from the Center, about sending a few students over to learn how to make paper. He referred us to the music teacher, who then brought a class to make paper and create a sculpture piece from the handmade paper.

Through this experience we learned that the person likely to know which students would benefit most from participation in art programming is not necessarily an administrator. The art, music or English-as-a-second-language teacher (or even a teacher's aide) might be the best resource for recruiting interested students.

The children from Vieau School enjoyed making paper, as did other neighborhood children who responded to a sign in the window inviting them to come in and make paper. Each day the Center was filled with children experiencing the joy of art.

At this time Elizabeth Austin, a Boston performance artist, was appearing at the Center. Her mix of homemade and conventional musical instruments offered a second foray into involving children in art experiences. The artist performed for groups of sixth grade students at the Center. She demonstrated how instruments such as a keyboard and handmade horns worked, and she allowed them to experiment with each instrument.

We were surprised at what we perceived to be a lack of attentiveness when the first group of kids kept whispering to each other as the artist spoke. The same thing happened with the afternoon group. We asked the teacher about this and learned that this was not disruptive or disrespectful behavior. The children, who came from various grade levels, were translating what the artist was saying from English to Spanish for their non-English speaking classmates.

Soon children began to stop by the Center on their way home after school. They were invited to watch artists set up exhibits and talk with them about the art. The kids volunteered to help stuff envelopes and do small errands. Many children were at first too shy to come in, but would peer through the big storefront windows at the art exhibits. These experiences proved so rewarding for the Center and the children that it was decided to provide art activities in a more organized way.

Local poet Ann Filemyr offered to teach poetry classes. She knew a teacher at an area school who would bring a few students to the Center. A grant from the Junior League enabled Ann to work with fifth graders from Allen-Field Elementary School each week for a semester. The children wrote beautiful and insightful poetry. Ann continued the program for a year and a half until she took a professorship in Ohio. She compiled some of the children's poetry into a booklet with a bright yellow cover. Ann wrote this dedication:

My Gift to You

Here it is
a small yellow book
yellow as the light of the sun
rising over Lake Michigan
sending shafts of yellow arrows
swift as your poems
on these pages.

You are my future
bright, hopeful as the sun
rising over Lake Michigan
shining on the face of children
reaching to sail in its light,
though often around you-
shadows of fallen factories
block out the sun.

Here it is
a brand new book
full of life
brilliant as your eyes
sparkling with first rays
at dawn on the waves of
Lake Michigan.   Ann Filemyr

One day while Ann was teaching a poetry class, Ellen Checota and Barbara Kohl-Spiro visited the Center to see about becoming involved. Seeing the enthusiasm and joy of the children touched both women. Ellen and Barbara are visual artists and immediately offered to teach a series of art classes. Within a few weeks after-school art classes were offered to the neighborhood children. The classes were free. Ellen and Barbara donated their time, came up with the project ideas and provided all the supplies.

Hands On was an immediate success. This drop-in program attracted 20 to 40 elementary school kids per session. Often, older siblings charged with taking care of their sisters and brothers would stay as well. The children didn't mind that the group had all ages from 6 through 12 and beyond. We observed that this is how these families took care of each other. A 12-year-old had no problem making art next to a 6- or 8-year-old.

Many of the children had little exposure to the arts either at school or at home; their families were not aware of them or they could not or did not feel comfortable visiting the art museum or other cultural opportunities in the city. Yet when given the opportunity and encouragement, the children created poignant work as they experienced the joy of creativity. They blossomed as they found the Center to be a safe haven for fun and learning.

We decided early on that we would not make any judgments as to the quality of a child's project—every project was good. Ellen and Barbara were very understanding with each child from interpersonal and creative standpoints. They did a variety of projects from hand-painted t-shirts to self-portraits, button art jewelry and painted landscapes.

Art classes were held in the gallery space. The children met and interacted with a variety of artists as they practiced for a performance or hung their work for an exhibit. Each artist was asked to take a few minutes to talk to the children about their work. Through these conversations the children developed a broad perspective about art and artists as they interacted with people from all over the world.

Ellen and Barbara gave a new vitality to the Center and planted the seeds for the Hands On program. The program took on a life of its own as it grew in importance for each child and for the spirit of the Center. Psychological and economic impacts were tremendous. The importance grew day by day, child by child. We did not realize just how significant this aspect of our programming had become until some time later.

As often happens in the non-profit world, the original supporters of the Center pulled out in 1989. The Board of Directors decided to move to another building about four blocks away. It was further from Vieau Elementary but within walking distance of Kagel Elementary School.

The new site required extensive remodeling, which was done through a non-profit training program and a significant contribution of volunteer labor. Architectural and design services to renovate the historic building were contributed by architect Pieter Yates Godfrey. Wisconsin Electric Power Company provided an in-kind grant valued at $20,000 for interior and exterior lighting.

During the renovation of the new location, the after-school art program continued, through the kindness of Father Bob Stiefrater, in the basement of Holy Trinity-Our Lady of Guadalupe Church. When the remodeling of the new site was complete, after-school art education became an integral part of the Center's total programming at the new location.

The Center applied for and received a grant from the Milwaukee Foundation for an art education Coordinator/Teacher. Receiving this grant was a vote of confidence and became the financial cornerstone for developing Hands On into a viable, ongoing program. We hired Christine Herrera, a poet of Colombian heritage. Her ability to speak Spanish was a definite plus with the high number of Hispanic children attending the program.

She introduced more Hispanic-related projects to celebrate and discuss. She recruited more children from area schools and taught classes two days a week after school in addition to helping with the weekly class given by Ellen and Barbara.

Barbara and Ellen set the tone for the Hands On art after-school program through warmth, fun, creativity and especially encouragement. Using the arts to bring joy and smiles for even a few hours a week gave hope and inspiration to children from many backgrounds and skill levels. Barbara spent time in Israel learning the methods used in the kibbutz to inspire hope and self-worth in children. She brought these skills to the after-school art program. After four years of setting the groundwork for the after-school art program, Barbara and Ellen went on to new endeavors.

Why call the program Hands On?

Christine Herrera, the first paid teacher, needed a title for the program for a grant she was writing. She thought about how she would begin a series of classes with the children by having them use a crayon to trace around their hands on paper. Each child would then be asked to tell a story about "Who I am" to the group. The hands were all different, just as each child was different. Yet the hands held many similarities as we all do, no matter how different we appear to be. The hands also symbolize how this program encourages the active participation in and involvement by many hands from young to old. It has been called Hands On ever since.

Early on we realized that to keep the program fresh, it is best to use a variety of artists as teachers. Artists can be great teachers. They offer a less structured approach and a fresher perspective. As the program grew in scope and numbers, it was necessary to have someone coordinate it, establish rules and expectations and integrate curriculum components to help reinforce science, language, math and other subjects. We learned that many of the children who attended sessions at the Center had little opportunity for help with homework at home. We collaborated with teachers in the area schools to present material through art that the children were talking about in their classrooms in order to reinforce academic ideas and concepts.

Artists who performed or exhibited at the Center were asked to talk to the children about their work as it progressed over several days because the children were curious about these people who spent days at the Center setting up art exhibitions or rehearsing for a performance. This interaction gave the children insight into the creative process and what is necessary to complete an art piece or plan a performance.

Most artists were willing to conduct a class in their specialty. Performers involved the children in creating a skit, using instruments or making costumes from simple materials. Visual artists used a variety of techniques with the children. Poets and writers helped the children write poetry and create personal books.

After seeing what an impact the artists had on the children, we included a paragraph in artist contracts requiring all artists who performed or exhibited at the Center to teach one or several classes at the Center or to do workshops at area schools.

Each artist decided what was most comfortable for him or her. Initially many artists were unsure about doing projects with children, but most found the experience not only enjoyable but enlightening as well. Due to the nature of their work or their personalities, some artists chose to work with older students at area high schools or alternative schools.

This outreach became so popular that several student classes a day attended artist workshops at the Center. Area schools appreciated the opportunity for their students to have a free or inexpensive art education outing. The children enjoyed learning something new in an exciting way.

Encouraging creativity in the children had a ripple effect, causing the minimal Center staff to find creative ways to fill staffing needs without having to raise the money to cover additional payroll. A successful development that increased the adult/student ratio without creating an impossible budget was

130

the use of college student interns. Students from area universities, colleges and institutes are a wonderful source of enthusiasm and energy. Not all the student interns worked directly with the children's art program, but all participated in some way.

As we became more successful in attaining grants and donations to fund the Hands On art program, it grew to four classes a week with special workshops and artist-in-residencies in collaboration with area schools. A summer program was initiated for six weeks, four days per week with two sessions per day.

Funding is an ongoing and crucial aspect of operating any after-school program. It took much effort to persuade funding sources that creating new projects or striving for larger budgets was not necessarily the way to go. There is a point when an organization realizes that it does not want to constantly increase budgets, staff, plans or location size. It is often best to get better at and improve upon what you do rather than trying to constantly expand.

A core group of foundations and individuals became our strongest supporters. They believed in the concept of using the arts to reach young people. They recognized the success and need for such programming and helped the Hands On program flourish through their financial assistance.

After four years of experience with the Hands On program, the Milwaukee Foundation held a series of sessions to evaluate the state of art education in the community outside of the school systems. They determined that the after-school art model using artists as teachers was a most innovative approach to reaching disadvantaged children. As a result of sharing this concept with other arts groups, the Milwaukee Repertory Theater hired a staff person to do community outreach and the Milwaukee Art Museum began an after-school art program in inner-city libraries.

Through sharing positive endeavors, other groups were sensitized to the need to help and the rewards of helping disadvantaged or underserved children get a better start in life by using the arts to develop skills, opportunities and personal enjoyment. Other organizations recognized the need for and importance of encouraging creativity while providing children a safe environment where they can just be kids.

18

Simple Art Projects

Fresh Fish Rubbings

Do not do this project if any children or adults are allergic to fish!

Supplies: One or more large, freshly killed and gutted fish
Bright latex or acrylic paints
Sheets of plain paper, cut larger than the fish
1" or 2" paint brushes
Newspaper

This project is not for the squeamish. However, even when the hesitant try it, they will have fun. Put cleaned fish onto a sturdy board or table covered with newspaper. Pat the fish dry with paper towels before brushing a coating of paint over the body. Position a sheet of paper over the painted fish's body and firmly press the paper on the fish. Use a finger to trace around the eye, mouth,

fins and gills. Gently peel off paper to reveal a dramatic fish portrait. Rinse fish with cool water and pat dry with paper towels before applying a different color paint.

Apply a layer of paint before each rubbing. Use several colors for a rainbow effect—like that of a rainbow trout. Make fish kites. Staple together two sheets of paper and stuff with crumpled newspaper to make a puffy fish.

Properly dispose of fish and thoroughly clean work area when done.

Sand Bottles

Supplies: Clean, dry, clear glass bottles
Fine sand (put beach sand through a sieve)
Funnel
Chop sticks, knitting needles, twigs
Colored chalk
Containers to hold colored sand
Corks or other stoppers to seal bottles

This project can be messy. Cover tables with paper or do the project on a paper-covered floor. Do not do this outside on a windy day.
- Have children separate chalk by color.
- Put pieces of one color between two pieces of heavy paper and pound the paper with smooth rocks, or use a grinding motion to pulverize the chalk. Blend portions of the pulverized chalk with portions of the plain sand to achieve the desired color.
- Mix small amounts of colored chalks together to make additional colors and then mix with sand.

Use a funnel to pour a layer of the colored sand into the bottle. Take a chopstick, wooden skewer, knitting needle or twig to poke down along the outer walls of the bottle to make wiggly or pointed designs in the sand at each level. Repeat, adding thick or thin layers of sand until you come to about one inch from the top. Be sure to seal each bottle securely!

While the children are grinding the chalk, mixing colors and filling the bottles, discuss where sand comes from and how it is sometimes used, such as for sandpaper and the bottles they are using. Discuss where chalk comes from.

This project encourages children to mix colored chalks to make new colors and to see how the desired color of sand is affected by the quantity of chalk used. Let creativity run wild. There is no right or wrong result. Add feathers to the top of the bottle. Make faces by gluing buttons to the outside of the bottle and adding bits of yarn for hair or other embellishments.

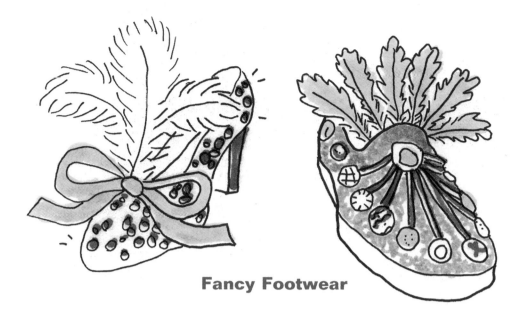

Fancy Footwear

Supplies: Inexpensive shoes from a resale store or
discount outlet
Glitter/feathers/buttons/ribbons/beads/shells/sequins
White glue
Sticks or old brushes to spread glue
Newspaper to cover table

Give each child one or two shoes to decorate in a fancy way. Spread the glue on only one side or section of the shoe at a time. Decorate with materials available. When finished, they have created an *objet d'art* to enjoy as a decorative piece or to clown around in.

Your Own Special Flag

Supplies: Colored stiff paper: construction or butcher paper
Scissors
Tape
Glue
Glitter/feathers/buttons/ribbons
Crayons or markers
Stapler
Coat hanger

Every country and state has its own flag. Design your special flag. Use a piece of paper as long as the coat hanger and fold the paper over the long bar of the hanger. Tape or staple the folded edge so it is secured over the hanger bar. Decorate the flag with colored paper cut into various shapes—stars, circles, triangles—and glue them on the flag. Use crayons or markers to draw extra designs. Add glitter, feathers, buttons or ribbons to add more pizzazz to your flag. Tie ribbons to the bottom to add flair. For even more zing, the teacher could spray paint the hangers bright colors before class.

Life-Size Personal Portraits

Supplies: Large roll or large sheets of craft paper
Scissors
Markers/pencils
Glue
Yarn/glitter/buttons/feathers
Colored paper, wallpaper or wrapping paper
Stapler and extra staples

Have child lie down on his/her back on a double thickness of craft paper. Have the teacher or another child trace the child's shape with a pencil or marker. Use scissors to cut out the shapes at least three inches larger than outline. Each child decorates himself or herself using markers to color in eyes, nose and mouth. Color in hair or use yarn to make the hairstyle. Color or cut clothing from colored paper, wallpaper or wrapping paper. Glue on buttons, glitter and feathers as desired.

Staple the decorated and plain sheets together, leaving a large enough opening to stuff the figure with crumpled newspaper and then staple the open end shut. Hang the group around the room to make a circle of friends.

Or have the children draw portraits of the mayor, school principal or other prominent people in your community to present to them or to do just for fun.

Portraits can be made flat using a single sheet of paper, but they are more fun stuffed.

Personal Paper Bag Pets

Supplies: Paper bags, one large and one small per animal
Construction paper (optional)
Pencil/markers
Hole punch
Tape
Newspaper
String

Fill one large and one small paper bag with crumpled newspaper. Stuff the top of the small bag into the top of the large bag. Tie string around both openings to make the animal's neck. For the animal's legs tear four (or however many) strips from a paper bag or construction paper and twist the strips or fold them into accordion folds and tape or staple them to the body. Cut paper shapes for ears and paper twists or pipe cleaners for whiskers or draw the animal's features with pencils and markers. Punch a hole at the top of the head and at the tail end. Tie a long piece of string through the holes at each end. Hold the string like a handle and take your pet for a walk. If you make more than one pet, parade around the block.

Gingerbread Park

Supplies: Graham crackers broken along perforated lines into squares
White and colored icing: homemade or store bought
Assorted candies: M&Ms, Life Savers, jelly beans,
chocolate pieces, jellied spearmint leaves, etc.
Assorted cereal squares, circles or flakes
Assorted uncooked noodle or macaroni shapes
Long licorice rods and strings in various colors
Shredded coconut
Pretzel rods

Note: Be sure to have plenty of goodies available for this project because many of the building materials are consumed before they reach the construction site!

Cut a 2'-square piece of heavy cardboard for each child. Use frosting to glue together four cracker squares to make a house in the park. Place the house on the cardboard, using frosting to secure it down. Before putting on the roof, decorate the walls with candy, cereal and pretzels. Use two more cracker sections to form a peaked roof over the house; use icing to attach roof at the peak and sides of the house. Let the icing set a few minutes before decorating the roof with chosen materials.

You can decorate the park, make flowers, trees, sidewalks, a swimming pool, play equipment and children playing—all out of the edible materials.

This project is often done in winter to simulate a winter scene. However, you can construct buildings, parks, a street in your town, etc., any time of year. Use different materials for trees, flowers, etc. to reflect the season.

Small Murals

Supplies: Sheet of plywood or foam core
Various colors of house or acrylic paints
Brushes in a variety of sizes
Colored markers
Rags for clean up
Old shirt smocks to protect clothing

Prepare the plywood or foam core by painting it a solid base coat. Create a fairy tale, folk tale or simple story mural and have the children design characters to go with a story. Have them paint the characters on the board in the order that they appear in the story so they can tell the story by simply pointing to the mural.

Class mural

Have the children depict a project that they did from beginning to end through a mural. They can embellish the work by adding materials they used in the project, such as glitter, feathers, buttons, etc. to give the work another dimension. Or unroll a roll of colored or plain brown craft paper at least 36" wide around the walls of a room. Position the bottom of the paper so that it is at a height even with the children's knees. At this height, the children can walk around the room painting, coloring and drawing in a story, map or designs. They can create a mural that surrounds them at a height that is easy to work on and appreciate.

Class portrait

Have the children draw portraits of each other or self-portraits by everyone in the group.

Do a mural of an area business

Have the children sketch out and then paint a portrait of a business. Paint the fruit and vegetable section of a local grocery, the candy counter at a drug store, customers in the chair at a barber or beauty shop or people doing laundry at a self-service laundry.

Checker Boards

Supplies: Square boards approximately 14" square x 1" thick
Rulers
Pencils
Paints of various colors
Brushes
Colored markers
Sand Paper
24 objects per board: flat stones, bottle caps, shells, etc.

Depending on the age of the children and tools and supervision available, show the children how to cut the wood. Be sure they are one-on-one with an adult at all times. Provide safety glasses and allow them to use only tools that have safety mechanisms in place. Have an adult smooth out jagged and rough areas and then teach the children to sand the flat surfaces and edges smooth.

Prepare the boards with a base coat of paint.

Divide the boards into a grid of 64 equal-size squares. Paint every other square one color, leave other squares plain and paint or decorate them in a contrasting color.

You need 24 game pieces per board. Use paint, markers or stickers on one side of each game piece so it can be turned over to use as a "king" in the game.

Note: Allow plenty of time to play a few games of checkers when the boards are finished.

chapter 19

Resources Available

Networking locally will lead you to people and resources to help establish and maintain a viable after-school art education program. As the need and effectiveness of after-school programs is increasingly documented, information on funding and research is more readily available.

Visit your public library or college and university libraries for information on this topic. Speak with educators at area colleges and school districts for input or suggestions. Meet with individual artists and professional artist organizations for information about art education programs they are involved in or know about in your state or region.

On the national level, several arts, education and youth-oriented organizations offer information, statistics, funding sources and links to programs throughout the United States. Visit the following Web sites for information on establishing and supporting nonprofit organizations, arts education, youth crime prevention, and intervention through the arts.

Funding Information Center Provides a bibliography and list of resources on how to start and operate nonprofit organizations in the United States.
www.mu.edu/fic/starting

Internet Nonprofit Center Provides a variety of resources for nonprofit organizations
www.nonprofits.org/lib/how.html

US Nonprofit Support Organizations Lists organizations by state that support and promote the work of community nonprofit groups.
www.idealist.org/support_states

Americans for the Arts Represents 3,800 local arts agencies. Includes data on grants and articles on the arts and at-risk youth.
www.artsusa.org

Arts Edge Offers support to the arts in the K-12 curriculum.
www.artsedge.kennedy-center.org

ArtsNet Links to agencies involved in the arts.
www.artsnet.heinz.cmu.edu

Catalog of Federal Domestic Assistance Provides government funding information
www.gsa.gov/fdac/queryfdac.htm

Coalition of Community Foundations for Youth Networks community foundations working to improve children's lives through safe spaces for kids.
www.ccfy.org

Coming Up Taller Describes over 200 out-of-school arts programs by state and discipline. (President's Committee on the Arts and Humanities)
www.cominguptaller.org

Connect for Kids Offers information-action center on children's issues, data on needs and examples of community initiatives.
www.connectforkids.org

Creative Partnerships for Prevention Offers resources on art-based drug and violence prevention for schools, cultural organizations and others working with youth.
www.CPPrev.org

The Foundation Center Online Acts as clearinghouse of information on foundations, corporate giving and other funding sources. Also available in hardcover in public and college or university libraries.
www.fdncetner.org

Gallery 37 Serves as a model for designing an arts-based, youth employment program. Located in Chicago, Illinois.
www.gallery37.org

National Endowment for the Arts Offers Grant information, news and links on the arts and arts education. Official web site of the NEA.
www.arts.endow.gov

National Endowment for the Humanities Official web site of NEH.
www.neh.gov

Nonprofit Gateway Provides links to federal government agencies.
www.nonprofit.gov

Start Smart Offers data on the arts in education and child development.
www.bravotv.com

National Assembly of State Arts Agencies Provides access to state arts agencies, some of which fund or operate art programs for children, news and links to various arts organizations.
www.nasa-arts.org

Urban Gateways Offers arts programs to public, private and parochial schools in Chicago and eight surrounding counties.
artsnet.heinz.cmu.edu/artsed/csgateways.html

National Art and Craft Suppliers:
Sax Arts and Crafts 800-558-6696
Dick Blick Art Materials 800-447-8192
Oriental Trading Company 800-228-2269

Appendix

Samples of flyers, letters and other materials are included in this Appendix to give you ideas on how to create effective documents for your organization. In addition there is a blank grant request application as well as a complete funding proposal and final report to help you prepare the information most often required by foundations and other funding organizations. Please do not reproduce any materials without the written permission of the authors.

- After school art program recruitment fliers
- Press clippings
- Fundraising party invitations
- Fundraising appeal letters
- Program update
- Letter of support from area school
- Thank you letters
- College intern request information
- Milwaukee Foundation Common Application
- Marshall Field's grant request and final report

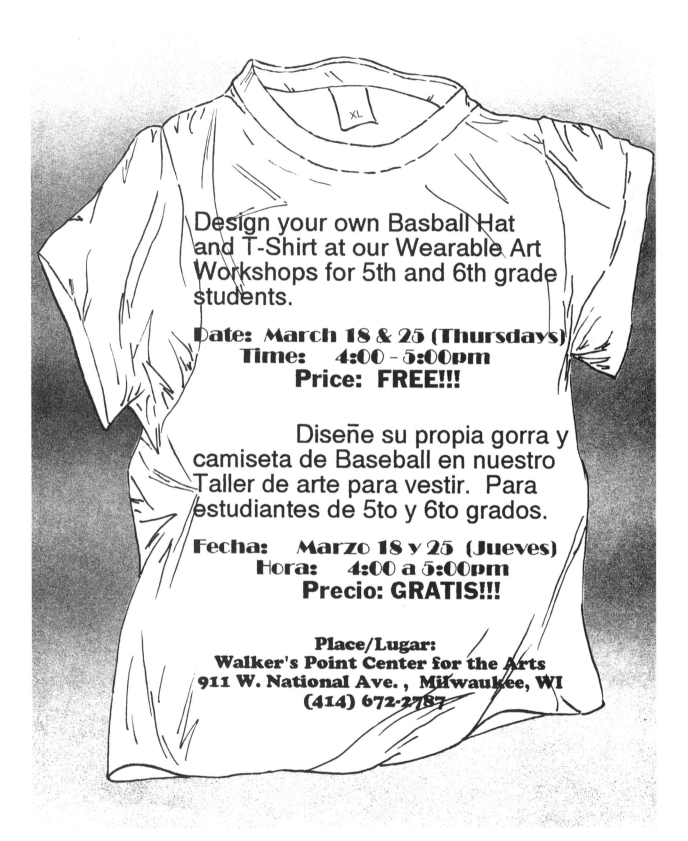

Design your own Basball Hat
and T-Shirt at our Wearable Art
Workshops for 5th and 6th grade
students.

Date: March 18 & 25 (Thursdays)
Time: 4:00 – 5:00pm
Price: FREE!!!

Diseñe su propia gorra y
camiseta de Baseball en nuestro
Taller de arte para vestir. Para
estudiantes de 5to y 6to grados.

Fecha: Marzo 18 y 25 (Jueves)
Hora: 4:00 a 5:00pm
Precio: GRATIS!!!

Place/Lugar:
Walker's Point Center for the Arts
911 W. National Ave. , Milwaukee, WI
(414) 672-2787

142

Winter Art Fun !

Join the Fun in January!

Free After-School Art Classes for Children
in grades 2-8.

In January we will be making Silly Snakes,
Mexican Yarn Paintings, miniature Costa
Rican Ox Carts, and Animalitos.

Wednesdays   3:00-4:30

Thursdays   4:30-5:30

For more information call Debbie at 672-2787.

****

Clases de Arte-Despres de la Escuela-Gratis
para nino y ninas de grades 2-8.

Miercoles   3:00-4:30

Jueves   4:30-5:30

WALKER'S POINT CENTER FOR THE ARTS
911 West National Avenue
672-2787

143

Milwaukee Sentinel

4A   MILWAUKEE SENTINEL   Saturday, July 23, 1994   ★ ★

Center introduces art to at-risk city children

By NANCY RAABE
Sentinel staff writer

"One small step for art, one giant step for mankind."

If Walker's Point Center for the Arts was immodest enough to have a motto, it might adopt that modification of Neil Armstrong's famous phrase.

As students of history know, the true measure of greatness lies not in a civilization's infrastructure or its low interest rates, but in the value it places on art.

"They say it's 'the arts,'" center curator and Director Jane Brite said during an interview in the small, sun-drenched garden behind the South Side storefront at 911 W. National Ave. "But I say it's prevention!"

Brite was referring to the center's commitment to saving low-income children from the ravages of teenage drug use, gangs, violence, crime and pregnancy by:

■ Developing their creativity, abilities and talent.

■ Encouraging them to express their feelings through art and language.

■ Giving them hope for a better future through exposure to the world outside their narrow environment.

Now in its fourth year, "Hands On" is a free, drop-in-after-school and summertime art program for low-income children.

The unique program provides neighborhood children ages 6 to 12 from Hispanic, black and Hmong backgrounds with 1 ½ hours of creative activity daily, four times a week. It runs for three weeks in the winter and six weeks in the summer.

Led by coordinator Lauren Hoke, intern Christina Cabarra and visiting guest artists, recent ventures included preparations by a group of talented older children for a mural at Our Lady of Guadalupe Church; the painting and humorous modification of two junk automobiles, donated by Esperanza Unida, for purposes of advertising and public art; tie-dying socks ("They love anything having to do with clothes," Brite said); hat decoration; and checkerboard making.

Brite said the program encouraged the children's confidence in artistic expression.

"Many are timid at the start, but because they come here and work with artists who think freely, when they approach a project at school, they're much more open about it," she said. "This is the incredible thing art can do for children. It brings out the creativity that we all have, but which these kids rarely have the chance to experience."

144

CATHOLIC HERALD

August 18, 1994 / 75¢   Archdiocese of Milwaukee   Vol. 125, No. 32 / 24 pages

MILWAUKEE – Muralist Ammar Tate puts the finishing touches on a mural near Trinity-Guadalupe Church, on city's south side. Youth from the parish and Walk- er's Point Center for the Arts designed the mural to cover up graffiti and show neighborhood unity. (Photo by James Pearson)

Graffiti-filled wall converted into mural

BY ANN BORGMANN

Catholic Herald Staff

MILWAUKEE – Alex Gonzalez, 17, envisions unity as a group of children swatting a piñata at a party.

His sister, Adriana, 15, believes dancing is what brings people together.

The two, who belong to Trinity-Guadalupe Parish, used those ideas to help a group of youth transform a graffiti-filled wall near the church into a colorful mural that illustrates neighborhood unity.

The mural will be officially dedicated Sunday after the 11 a.m. Mass.

The parish had been planning to paint the wall for two years – "since I got here,"

said youth minister Eddie Gutierrez. The project was a collaborative effort between the parish, 613 S. 4th St., and Walker's Point Center for the Arts, which received a grant to train kids to paint murals.

Walker's Point hired Ammar Tate, a muralist, to oversee the design and recruited some youth from the neighborhood. The entire job took about four weeks, according to Kat Hendrickson, assistant curator at Walker's Point. No spray paint was used.

The finished product is a collage depicting the neighborhood's mostly Latino culture. Among other things, it shows children hitting a piñata, a mother embracing her son, a woman dancing with a

skeleton and a man making an offering to Our Lady of Guadalupe. Embracing all are the wounded hands of Christ.

"We just kind of let the kids create what they thought would be a positive image of the neighborhood," Gutierrez said.

He said Our Lady of Guadalupe was featured prominently because she is the parish's patron saint. The skeleton is a symbol for death, which isn't a frightening thing in Latino culture.

"The basic statement is that she's been with us in our joy and our sorrow," Gutierrez said.

He said the parish might paint a poem or prayer on the part of the wall that

wasn't used.

Support from neighbors and parishioners has been overwhelming, according to Hendrickson. "It was amazing once we started working out there how many people stopped and got out of their cars and started talking to us."

Hendrickson said she tried to urge youth who were watching to paint a little. The more people involved in the project, she figured, the less chance it would be ruined by gangs.

"They did a very nice job," remarked Pat Hach, whose sister, Alice Ledesma, owns the nearby Lunch Box Catering.

Walker's Point puts back yard in order

Center for the Arts turns to the beauty that flourishes out of doors

By EDITH BRIN
of The Journal staff

A TREE GROWS in Walker's Point, and shrubs and flowers, too, as Jane Brite and company at the Walker's Point Center for the Arts create a teaching urban garden.

Here inner city kids can learn the joys of the soil and the smell of the lilacs.

"Otherwise, these kids don't see flowers," says Brite, director of the center.

The 30-foot-wide back yard (to stretch the meaning of the word yard) at 911 W. National Ave. wasn't much to look at till now. In fact, it was a distinctly tacky mess of dirt, leaves, gravel and discarded building materials.

But great promise blooms.

Brite's helpers — education coordinator Sherrill Weller, along with a University of Wisconsin-Milwaukee intern and a volunteer — scratched up donations of landscape designs, planters, plants, paving materials and more, and are well under way.

Their plan includes a layout in patio stone of the 42 numbered plots that make up Walker's Point, so that the children can identify where they live, Brite says.

Also envisioned — some of it, they hoped, to be in place by tonight, when an open house introduces the garden to the Friends of Walker's Point — are borders of trees and shrubs. Ultimately, the 30-by-45-foot space should feel totally enclosed.

Old pavers from National Ave. found buried on the property are being used. Other materials include new bricks and wood chips.

Scented garden beds for the kids to experience will hold lilac, peony, lavender, peppermint, sage, chives and thyme. Movable tables will accommodate art classes in the garden. Raised vegetable beds are also in the works.

Children who are part of the Center's Hands-On Program already have planted seeds in pots and are keeping things watered.

Donations of plants, shrubs, garden tools or supplies will be gratefully accepted, Brite says. She can be reached at 672-2787.

PLEASE JOIN US TO UNVEIL STAGE 1 OF
WPCA'S NEW URBAN GARDEN.

The garden is "in progress." Staff and
volunteers have been collecting
supplies for the project. A UWM
School of Architecture student
helped design the plan and a
horticulturist suggested
plantings for the garden.

◆

The garden will be used by the
children who take part in our
free Hands-On art program. The
children planted seeds, are watering
the plants that are emerging and will
be carrying on their art projects in their
new garden. Some classes will be based upon
the flora and fauna of our garden.

◆

Receptions for members and special guests will be held in the
garden which we hope will grow and blossom into a secluded
sanctuary in the midst of the hustle and bustle of city life.

◆

Please join us for a light buffet of tasty
delights and refreshments.
A $5.00 donation per person is
requested. If you have a plant,
shrub, garden tool or supplies that
you would like to donate to the
garden, please bring it along.

◆

The opening of Mark McGinnis'
"Wonderful World of Explorers",
featuring his illustrated lecture
will be held at 6:30 pm.

WALKER'S POINT

The pleasure of your company

is requested

at a fund raising event for

Walker's Point Center for the Arts

•

Saturday, August 13th

7:00 O'Clock p.m.

1469 East Lilac Lane

Fox Point

WOOF

Please join this eclectic group of hosts
for an unusually delightful evening
to help a particularly important cause.

IT'S A PARTY

•

Saturday, August 13, 1994

7:00 p.m.

Sally's home and interior designer were featured
in the April issue of Milwaukee Magazine

1469 East Lilac Lane
Fox Point, Wisconsin

•

Summer Buffet

•

Celebrity Doodle Auction

Featuring the Doodles of Artists, Politicians, Statesmen (depending upon you point of view),
the Rich & Famous (not to mention Infamous), Sports Figures,
Television Personalities, Writers and many others.
Doodle frames will be hand decorated b y the children in our
Hands On After School Children's Program.

•

Music by Random Walk

Summer Casual Attire

FANCY SCHMANCY!!

WALKER'S POINT CENTER for the ARTS

in Fox Point

WALKER'S POINT CENTER FOR THE ARTS

911 WEST NATIONAL AVENUE

MILWAUKEE, WISCONSIN 53204

414-672-2787

September, 1993

WPCA Hands On Update

The Tuesday, Wednesday and Thursday Hands On after school art classes are experiencing a record enrollment. Some of our "regulars" are back, but we also have many new young faces. Enthusiasm on the part of the teachers and kids is high.

The beginning sessions focused on enjoying Al Balinsky's summer photography project (done by Hands On participants from our neighborhood) entitled "Our Global Community".

Several classes were devoted to making sculptures in the style of Marian Vieux and learning about her "wrap" technique. We hung the "masterpieces" created by the children in our front windows.

The children are currently working with local artist, Carrie Skoczek, in three mask making activities: painted screen masks, paper bag masks decorated with feathers and ribbon, and cardboard build-up masks.

October activities will center around the *Dia De Los Muertos* (*Day of the Dead*) exhibition which opens on October 31.

Thank you for your support of Hands On. Your support gives these children an opportunity to experience the arts in ways they would never dream possible.

Sincerely,

Jane Brite	Barbara Niggemann	Marlene Jaglinski
Director	Education Coordinator	Administrator

WALKER'S POINT CENTER FOR THE ARTS

911 WEST NATIONAL AVENUE

MILWAUKEE, WISCONSIN 53204

414-672-2787

June 29, 2000

Dear Mrs. Smith,

School is out for the summer and good kids make bad decisions when they do not have direction and a chance to direct their energy in a positive way. Through "Hands On", our summer art program for the low income and primarily Hispanic kids of the Walker's Point neighborhood, we hope to keep 250 children active and productive while they have fun this summer.

These 250 kids will be in a safe setting and will participate in projects about the rain forest, life in the circus and wearable art. They will enforce their reading, writing, math and science skills as each project will integrate these subjects.

Our summer program began June 20 with "Hands On" resources that are just about used up due to program demands throughout the school year. Success is great, but more kids mean more supplies, more snacks and more teacher hours. Please help us keep "Hands On" running throughout the summer. Each class session for 30 kids costs us $100 per day for teachers, supplies and nutritious snacks.

Can you make any contribution toward continuing "Hands On" this summer? A donation of $25.00 or any amount you choose will help bring smiles and opportunities to 250 beautiful children.

Sincerely,

Jane Brite
Director

MILWAUKEE PUBLIC SCHOOLS

ALBERT E. KAGEL SCHOOL

1210 West Mineral Street
Milwaukee, Wisconsin 53204-2192
Area 414: 647-1552

March 25, 1992

Ms. Jane Brite
Walkers Point Center for the Arts
907 W. National Ave.
Milwaukee, WI 53204

Dear Ms. Brite:

I am writing this letter to express my appreciation for the wonderful opportunities and programs WPCA has provided for our students. The after-school program is a rare opportunity for students to explore their creativity and expand their minds. The importance and significance of this program is evidenced by the continued enthusiastic participation of the students.

In addition to the after-school program, the classroom field trips that provide opportunities to work with visiting artists are excellent for various reasons. Children from this area would not have this kind of exposure to such a variety of people without this program. Artists from Mexico, Puerto Rico and other countries not only broaden students' horizons but also produce a sense of self-esteem and pride as excellent role models of their cultures. The type of shows and exhibits are always relevant to the cultural background of the area.

You offer an important and unfortunately, seldom provided, role in the development of our students that cannot be replaced by the schools. We are very fortunate to be able to work with you. Thank you.

Sincerely,

Ms. Rose Guajardo, Principal
Albert E. Kagel Elementary

RG/lb

WALKER'S POINT CENTER FOR THE ARTS

911 WEST NATIONAL AVENUE

MILWAUKEE, WISCONSIN 53204

414-672-2787

November 1, 1997

Dear Mr. and Mrs. Jaglinski,

We're going to Walker's Point to "Get Art"

That's what a group of fifth graders, merrily trekking along National Avenue, replied when they were asked where they were so happily going. What a great endorsement for Hands On, our after school art classes, for the low income children who live in the Walker's Point area.

Since 1987 Hands On has grown from a handful of children who would wander into the gallery to a formal arts program involving over 600 children in our after school and summer classes. The arts reach another 2,000 children through our collaborative and cooperative art education programming with neighborhood schools. Without Hands On these children would receive only minimal exposure to the arts. This is unfortunate because the arts have been proven to stimulate creativity, aid the understanding of other subjects and most importantly, enhance self-esteem.

Children who reside in the Walker's Point area are faced with many negative choices including gangs and drugs. Through the arts and the individual attention they receive in Hands On classes, these children blossom and become expressive and self-assured.

I am writing to ask for your support for this unique after school art program at Walker's Point Center for the Arts. Your donation of $25 will help to:

- Provide nutritious snacks for the children before classes
- Defray the costs of art materials
- Underwrite the fees for the professional arts hired to teach the classes

With your help many children will have a place to be safe, creative and happy when they "get art".

Sincerely,

Jane Brite
Director

WALKER'S POINT CENTER FOR THE ARTS

911 WEST NATIONAL AVENUE

MILWAUKEE, Wisconsin 53204

414-672-2787

May 13, 1993

Jeraldine Marchart
Milwaukee Board of Realtors
Youth Foundation, Inc.
P.O. Box 1375
Milwaukee, WI 53213

Dear Ms. Marchart,

Enclosed are some recent photographs and a narrative describing our after school
art program at Walker's Point Center for the Arts. As always, you, or a
representative from your Board are welcome to visit the Center to sit in on a Hands
On class.

We thank you for your support and wish to express our gratitude for your concern
and efforts on behalf of area youth. It is through the social awareness of
organizations like yours that we can work together to help young people become
happy and productive adults.

Sincerely,

Barbara Niggemann
Education Coordinator

Enc.

WALKER'S POINT CENTER FOR THE ARTS

911 WEST NATIONAL AVENUE

MILWAUKEE, WISCONSIN 53204

414-672-2787

December 20, 1997

Dear Mr. and Mrs. Ruiz,

On behalf of Walker's Point Center for the Arts and in particular the children who attend Hands On, our after school art education program, we wish to express our gratitude for your donation of $100.00 toward this worthwhile program.

We would also like to invite you to visit WPCA to see our ever-changing exhibits, attend a wide array of performances and visit with the children who come to Hands On classes to see how their involvement in the arts has had a positive impact on their lives.

Sincerely,

Jane Brite

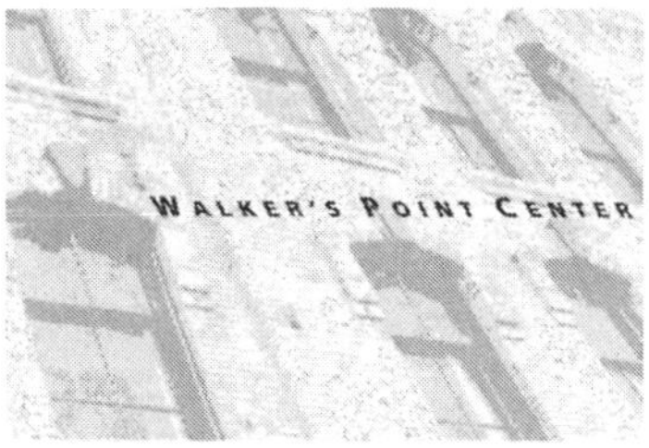

WALKER'S POINT CENTER FOR THE ARTS
911 WEST NATIONAL AVENUE
MILWAUKEE, WISCONSIN 53204
414-672-2787

August 8, 2000

Inga Zile
Art Department
Fine Arts Center
University of Wisconsin - Milwaukee
PO Box 413
Milwaukee, WI 53201

Dear Ms. Zile,

We are currently interviewing students for internships for the fall semester. Interns at Walker's Point Center for the Arts get experience in and learn about the many aspects of a non-profit, multi-disciplinary, multi-cultural art center.

WPCA offers interns experience in:

- **public and media relations**
- **exposure to art education classes with children from various social, economic and ethnic backgrounds**
- **publicity**
- **grant writing**
- **performance**
- **exhibit presentations**
- **curatorial opportunities**

Please encourage your students to take advantage of this internship opportunity which will benefit them in their course work and career choices. Interested students should call WPCA to set up an interview.

Sincerely,

Jane Brite
Director

enclosure

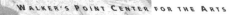

WALKER'S POINT CENTER FOR THE ARTS

911 WEST NATIONAL AVENUE

MILWAUKEE, Wisconsin 53204

414-672-2787

You Can Make A Difference Through the Arts

Whatever your vocation or avocation:

Education, Public Relations, Curatorial, Sound or Visual Technician

Walker's Point Center for the Arts volunteer opportunities:

+ give you hands on **experience** to beef up your resume,
+ give you practical **behind the scenes knowledge,**
+ give you a chance to see first hand how **the arts can effect everyone** in a community from six to sixty!

Flexible hours and projects.

WPCA is conveniently located at 911 W. National with a bus stop right outside our door.

For more information call

Walker's Point Center for the Arts — 672-2787.

COMMON APPLICATION FORM

Provide the following grant information in this order. For your convenience, you may choose either to copy and fill out this cover summary or to create your own using the headings listed below.

Funder applying to: _____   Date Submitted: _____

Total Proposed Project/Program Budget: _____   Amount Requested: _____

Program Name: _____

Duration of Project/Program: from: _____   to: _____

When are funds needed? _____

Nature of Request: ___ capital request ___ project ___ operating ___ program ___ other

```
┌─────────────────────────────────────────────────────────────────────────────┐
│ Organization Information:                                                     │
│ Name and address:                                                             │
│                                                                               │
│                                                                               │
│                                                                               │
│ Phone number: _____  TTY: _____  FAX number: _____ │
└─────────────────────────────────────────────────────────────────────────────┘
```

Chief Staff Officer: _____   Phone number: _____

Contact Person/Title: _____   Phone number: _____

Board Chairperson: _____

Date of establishment: _____

Dates of organization's fiscal year: _____

Organization's total operating budget for past year _____ and current year _____

Has the governing board approved a policy which states that the organization does not discriminate as to age, race, religion, sex or national origin? yes ____ no ____

Does the organization have federal tax exempt status? yes ____ no ____ If no, please explain:

Has this request been authorized by the organization's governing body?   yes ____ no ____ When? _____

This application must be signed by an officer of the organization's governing body:

_____   _____
Signature   Title

Submit the following attachments with the completed proposal:

1. Complete list of the organization's officers and directors
2. The organization's actual income and expense statement for the **past** fiscal year, identifying the organization's principal sources of support
3. The organization's projected income and expense budget for the **current** fiscal year, identifying the projected revenue sources
4. The organization's most recent audited financial statement including notes and IRS Form 990
5. Copies of the IRS federal tax exemption determination letters

NARRATIVE

PLEASE PROVIDE THE FOLLOWING INFORMATION IN NARRATIVE FORM IN THIS ORDER. NOTE SECTIONS THAT ARE NOT REQUIRED FOR REQUESTS FOR GENERAL OPERATING SUPPORT.

(5 pages maximum)

Project/Program Abstract

Provide a brief summary of the proposed project/program including:
- project/program outcomes and strategy for achieving them;
- total estimated costs;
- the amount requested from this funder and how the funds will be used;
- other principal sources of support.

Organization Information

Provide a brief summary of the organization's:
- mission and goals, and major accomplishments;
- description of the population served, including total number and other important characteristics;
- principal geographic area served;
- total number of paid staff and volunteers.

Project/Program Description (not required for general operating requests)

- Specify project/program outcomes that you plan to achieve.
- Who and how many will be served and why are you serving them? Why would they use your particular services? What geographic area does this project/program target?
- How will you reach the population you plan to serve? How will you involve this population in the design and implementation of the project/program?
- What strategies will be used to achieve the proposed outcomes? Include any linkages or collaborations with other organizations and how they will help to achieve outcomes.
- How will you know if you have achieved the outcomes proposed (how will progress be tracked and outcomes measured) and how will you use that information to make changes if needed?

Capacity to Carry Out Program (not required for general operating requests)

- Describe qualifications of staff/volunteers responsible for the project/program.
- Describe the organization's commitment to the project/program and the people whom it will benefit.
- How does the project/program relate to the organization's mission?

Funding Considerations (not required for general operating requests)

Describe plans for obtaining other funding needed to carry out the project/program, including amounts requested of other funders. If the project/program is expected to continue beyond the grant period describe plans for ensuring continued funding after the grant period.

Common Application

If you are requesting general operating support, do not complete this form, but send total agency budget, or capital budget if you are requesting capital support.

PROJECT/PROGRAM BUDGET

ORGANIZATION NAME: _____

....

REVENUE

	Total Revenue	Committed	Pending
1. United Way Allocation	$ _____	$ _____	$ _____
2. Other Federated Campaign Allocations	_____	_____	_____
3. Contracts (list specific sources on following page)	_____	_____	_____
4. Grants (list specific sources on following page	_____	_____	_____
5. In-Kind Support (list specific sources on following page)	_____	_____	_____
6. Client and Program Service Fees and Other Earned Revenue	_____	_____	_____
7. Contributions	_____	_____	_____
8. Other Revenue (list specific sources on following page)	_____	_____	_____
TOTAL PROJECT/PROGRAM REVENUE	$ _____	$ _____	$ _____

EXPENSES

1. Salaries (provide detail by position on a separate page, <u>except for United Way applications</u>	$ _____
2. Benefits/Taxes	_____
3. Professional Fees	_____
4. Supplies, Printing, Duplicating	_____
5. Travel	_____
6. Telephone	_____
7. Occupancy	_____
8. Payments to Affiliates	_____
9. Major Property & Equipment Acquisition	_____
10. Other Expenses	_____
11. Allocation of support service costs to program <u>(United Way application only)</u>	_____
TOTAL PROJECT/PROGRAM EXPENSES	$ _____

PROJECT/PROGRAM REVENUE SUPPLEMENT
(Please indicate revenue sources as committed or pending)

Contracts (list)	Total Revenue	Committed	Pending
_____	_____	_____	_____
_____	_____	_____	_____
_____	_____	_____	_____
_____	_____	_____	_____
_____	_____	_____	_____
_____	_____	_____	_____
_____	_____	_____	_____
_____	_____	_____	_____

Grants (list)

_____	_____	_____	_____
_____	_____	_____	_____
_____	_____	_____	_____
_____	_____	_____	_____
_____	_____	_____	_____
_____	_____	_____	_____
_____	_____	_____	_____
_____	_____	_____	_____

In-Kind Support (list)

_____	_____	_____	_____
_____	_____	_____	_____
_____	_____	_____	_____
_____	_____	_____	_____
_____	_____	_____	_____
_____	_____	_____	_____
_____	_____	_____	_____

Other (list)

_____	_____	_____	_____
_____	_____	_____	_____
_____	_____	_____	_____
_____	_____	_____	_____
_____	_____	_____	_____
_____	_____	_____	_____

GLOSSARY

Outcome - The intended impact or results a program or project is trying to produce.

Project - A planned undertaking or organized set of services designed to achieve specific outcomes that begins and ends within the grant period. (Note: a successful project may become an ongoing program of the organization.)

Program - An organized set of services designed to achieve specific outcomes for a specified population that will continue beyond the grant period.

Capital Request - A planned undertaking to purchase, build or renovate a space or building or to acquire equipment.

General Operating Support - Grant funds to support the ongoing services, mission or goals of an organization.

March 24, 1993

Community Relations Specialist
Marshall Field's
111 N. State Street
Chicago, Illinois 60602

Dear Community Relations Specialist,

Walker's Point Center for the Arts (WPCA), an established venue for visual and performing artists, and Kagel School, a public elementary school serving over 350 culturally and ethnically diverse students, request funding assistance for a collaborative artist-in-residence paper making project.

Students at Kagel School are: Hispanic, 75%; white 11%; Asian, 10%; African American, 3%; and Native American, 1%. Kagel School is located in Walker's Point, a low- income area of Milwaukee targeted for revitalization. WPCA is a non-profit art center presenting quality visual and performance artists of regional, national and international renown. WPCA chooses to remain in an under served area of the city and actively participates in the economic and social growth of the community through the arts. All artists at the center participate in community outreach through Hands On, free after school art classes for the neighborhood children, or through workshops at area schools.

Due to budget and staffing restraints, children in area schools have only minimal exposure to the arts. This is unfortunate because it is proven that through comprehensive programs and curriculum integration the arts can stimulate a child's creativity, aid in the understanding of other subjects and most importantly for these children, enhances their self-esteem. Drugs and gangs are pervasive forces on children in this area. Through the arts they can express their feelings in non-judgmental ways allowing even those with language barriers an opportunity for expression.

Kagel School does not have space to host a paper maker. Therefore, a partnership between Kagel and WPCA is an ideal cooperative effort. The students will walk to WPCA for the actual paper making process.

WPCA's Education Coordinator and the administration at Kagel School planned the project and agreed that hosting a paper maker would benefit all students and enable the teachers to integrate paper making into curriculum areas associated with science and the environment. Discussions and projects will stress using found objects and recycling materials into new useful and/or art forms.

Students will work directly with artist Kirsten Christianson who will show them her hand made paper books and lamps to demonstrate how art can have decorative, functional and fun applications. Artist Christianson was chosen because she is experienced in communicating and presenting engaging experiences for children. She is registered as a prominent artist in residence with the Wisconsin Arts Board.

The cultural and ethnic diversity of the school will be discussed and the children will be asked to include small items that reflect their heritage in a hand made paper mural. Total student participation will be stressed because making paper is an opportunity for all the children to work together on a project that does not reflect a particular culture or heritage. "At-risk" students will be targeted for a core group as we have found that these children are often looking for a positive way to express themselves and when given the opportunity they will go beyond all expectations. Positive feedback will increase their interest in learning and help keep them in school.

Kagel School parents, staff and the general public will be invited to attend a paper making session at WPCA. WPCA is recognized as a presenter of quality arts programming for the diverse audiences of southeastern Wisconsin. This collaborative effort will further our mission to be an active and contributing community partner.

At the end of the residency an exhibit of the children's work will be held at WPCA. After the public exhibit, selected pieces by the children and the mural they create will be on permanent display at Kagel School. This collaborative program will cost $2,690. Over 375 students will have an engaging educational experience to see how to participate in the arts as individuals as well as how the arts can affect our surroundings and impact our lives. Funding consideration for this project will serve Kagel School students with a program they would otherwise not be able to experience.

Please contact us should you need any further information regarding this collaborative artist in residence proposal.

Sincerely,

Jane Brite

Jane Brite
Director
Enc.

Marshall Field's

GRAND AVENUE MALL
101 W. WISCONSIN AVE. • MILWAUKEE, WI 53260-0001

October 21, 1993

Ms. Jane Brite
Director
Walker's Point Center for the Arts
911 West National Avenue
Milwaukee, WI 53204

Dear Jane:

Marshall Field's is pleased to announce a grant to the Walker's Point Center for the Arts for the 1993 fund campaign. We are delighted to be able to provide this support. Enclosed is an invitation for Monday, November 1, 1993, at which time we will present the check for $2,700.00.

Enclosed are two Agreement with Grantee forms. Please sign both copies and return one to Kassie Davis, Public Affairs Director, Marshall Field's, 111 North State Street, Chicago, IL 60602. The other copy is for your records. Please identify our company as "Marshall Field's" in announcement or recognition of our grant.

We are hopeful that our grant will provide support to further the important work of the Walker's Point Center for the Arts and hope that 1993 will bring added success to its worthwhile efforts.

Sincerely,

Debra Kavanaugh

Debra Kavanaugh
Store Manager

DK:mm

Enclosures

COMMUNITY GIVING PROGRAM GRANTEE REPORT-- 1993

(Please type and limit narrative to space provided. Please fill in completely and do not use "see attacted.")

Organization Name ___Walker's Point Center for the Arts___

Address ___911 W. National Avenue___

City, State, Zip ___Milwaukee, WI   53204___

Contact/Title ___Jane Brite, Director___

Phone ___414-672-2787___

> **DUE WITHIN
> 12 MONTHS OF GRANT**
>
> Must be returned before
> application for renewal of
> grant will be accepted.

Date Awarded __11-1-93__ $__2,700__ for __Papermaking Workshop Artist-in-Residence__

Results expected: (from original application)
Please list results you expected to achieve:

1. Provide a needed service to Kagel School.

2. Integrate the arts into the school curriculum in the areas of science and math.

3. Positive experience for the children.

Please state how you knew if you achieved each result:

1. Entire staff, students and many parents were involved with project and academic spin-offs.

2. Several teachers used the paper making techniques to talk about recycling, forests and use of nature in a positive way.

3. Many children who came with Kagel School also attended extra sessions at the Center & brought their friends.

Actual Results: (what actually happened, what was accomplished, what wasn't, what problems did you encounter?)

The 59 5th graders at this school are considered "at risk" because they are at an age where they can be easily seduced by the negative influences of the streets. As a result, they received intensive exposure in the papermaking workshop so they can be reminded how important staying in school is by relating school work to everyday life. The workshop achieved this goal because the children who have a hard time staying on task with their regular school work participated with full attention and enthusiastically throughout the workshop. They were amazed at the pulp process, seeing waste paper and throw away items turned into a beautiful mural. All students were involved in this project in some way. The mural toured the school as several of the 5th graders took it into each classroom to explain what they did and about the workshop. The mural and work by several of the students is on permanent display in the school library. The only improvement would be to have additional adults at each session.

Conclusions: (based on your results thus far, how will you change this program to improve the outcome?)

Collaboration with the school and artist with WPCA staff went very well. The students were excited and enthusiastic about the project and the resultant mural. Many invited their friends and family to see the papermaking at WPCA. The teachers integrated the concepts of science and math used in paper and mural making into their curriculum as a spin off of the project. The only suggestion to improve the outcome would be to have had additional adults to allow the children to work in smaller groups.

Printed on recycled paper

166

Summary of project budget: (please list major categories of expense and amounts budg...)

```
Artist Fee ( 6 days x $250)              1500.00
Project Supplies ($100 x 6 days)          600.00
Education  Coordinator                    600.00
Bi-lingual Aid                            600.00
                                         _____
Total                                   $3300.00*
```

*Total does not include in-kind contributions by WPCA for space, insurance, administration of the project or release time or preparation time by teachers involved.

Summary of Financial Data -- Total Organization:

REVENUE	Budget/Current Fiscal Year Ending 1/31/94 $	%	Actuals/Most Recently Completed Fiscal Year Ending 1/31/93 $	%
Earned	22000	7	15414	8
Foundations/Corporations	57000	51	57245	50
Individuals	5000	3	4000	3
Government	31000	30	34470	30
United Way	-	-	-	-
Special Events/Other	13000	9	12035	9
Investment Income	-	-	-	-
Total	128,000	100%	123,164	100%

EXPENSES

Program	71000	56	68340	52
Administrative	54000	40	50749	43
Development	3000	4	2500	5
Total	128,000	100%	121,589	100%
Excess (Deficiency)			1,575+	
Beginning Fund Balance				
Ending Fund Balance				

Top Five Corporate Donors to Organization & Amounts (most recent fiscal year):

1. Pettit Foundation	$	20,000
2. Mc Donald's Children Fdn.	$	10,000
3. Kohler Fdn.	$	3,500
4. Marshall Field's	$	2,700
5. Milwaukee Realtors	$	2,500

Top Five Confirmed Donors to Project & Amounts (current fiscal year):

1. Milwaukee Foundation	$	10,000
2. WI Arts Board	$	7,000
3. Kohler Fdn.	$	5,000
4. Quadracci's	$	2,500
5. Woman's Club	$	1,500

Checklist of Required Attachments:

[ ] List of officers and directors of the organization and their affiliations
[ ] Copy of most recent IRS tax exempt certificate
[ ] Audited financial statement for the most recent fiscal year
[ ] Organization budget for current year including anticipated expenses and income sources
[ ] Completed 1993 Grantee report - only for organizations receiving a grant in 1992 from Dayton's, Hudson's or Marshall Field's
[ ] Qualitative Criteria Narrative – Marshall Field's _only_
[ ] Optional - Additional information on proposed project and its budget
[ ] Optional - Most recent organization Annual Report

Marshall Field's Paper Making Project Questions

1. Please describe the paper making project residency.

The paper making residency is designed with two aspects of community outreach in mind.

A. The Artist will work with students and teachers at Kagel School.

Kagel School and WPCA have developed a unique relationship. Students at the school have minimal exposure to the arts. However, Kagel staff recognize the importance and significance of the arts in the lives of the children and to their overall development. They have therefore, encouraged their students to attend our free after school art classes and have welcomed artists who perform or exhibit at WPCA to speak to, or perform for their students either at the school or have walked their students to WPCA.

Project Structure

First, the artist will meet with Kagel staff to explain what the project is and what she would like to see accomplished in terms of having the children learn about the use and re-use of objects - recycling. Then she will take recycling one step further to create new products and art from the recycled materials. She will integrate the recycling of paper products, use of fibers from old clothing and fabrics commonly found in any household, the use of old jewelry, buttons, ribbon, etc. into the paper making project. The recycling aspect will fit in with the science and math curriculum. Kagel teachers will also be encouraged to emphasize the various aspects of recycling in their English classes.

Secondly, the artist will work with students, teachers and parents at Kagel to give a general overview of the project, the history of paper making, techniques the children will be learning. She will show them samples of paper making projects that have been done at other schools. All students will come to the Center to see a demonstration on how the pulp is screened and the paper set and will have an opportunity to actually make their own paper.

Students in the 5th and 6th grades will spend more time on the project than the younger children. They will create a mural of hand made paper which will first be on display at Walker's Point Center for the Arts during our Ecology exhibit which will be open for the entire Milwaukee community to see. After this it will be mounted for permanent display at Kagel School.

B. The artist will work with children at WPCA's "Hands On" after school art program.

WPCA does extensive community outreach in the neighborhood through "Hands On", our free summer and after school art program for neighborhood children. This past summer a record number of almost 300 children attended our six week summer session. "Hands On" classes are taught by professional artists within WPCA's gallery space. The children are therefore encouraged to be creative while surrounded by an ever changing array of work by professional artists.

Children who attend "Hands On" after school classes come from various area schools. Some area children are bussed to schools outside the neighborhood, but come WPCA classes when they return home. The children come from Hispanic, African American, Asian and American Indian, low income households. Many of the schools that the children attend have minimal art programs, so the children really relish the opportunity to be creative in a non-judgmental setting. Even those who have a language other than English as their primarily language, can participate in the classes without a language barrier. Our Education Coordinator reads to the children at some time during each class. She reads a story in English and will ask for volunteers to translate the story for the children who may not fully understand it.

WPCA deliberately keeps classes small and selects artists to work with the children based upon their ability to not only share their work and encourage creativity, but also how well they can relate to the children and are willing to serve as mentors to them. So many of the children do not have someone to freely talk to about fears and problems, their hopes and dreams. WPCA allows the children an opportunity to talk to caring adults while they do their projects.

The children who attend "Hands On" will also learn the history, recycling aspects and techniques of paper making. They will work with the artist over a period of three weeks and also create hand made paper sculpture and mural pieces to be hung in the gallery during the Ecology Exhibition.

2. How was Kagel School chosen

Two years ago, WPCA did a similar project with Vieau School, another area school. The project received much publicity and the staff at Kagel asked if we could collaborate with them to repeat the project with their students. The biggest problem for both the school and WPCA is the funding of the artist's residency and materials. WPCA therefore initiated the request for funds to Marshall Field's. Kagel School, through their parent group, will supply the extra volunteers needed to help the children during the paper making workshop and in the classrooms with extra class projects related to the artist in residency. The Kagel staff has been supportive of WPCA activities and appreciates our presence in the community.

3. Did WPCA solicit input from school staff?

Yes, Barbara Niggemann, WPCA's Education Coordinator, met several teachers and school administrators to review the idea and collaborate on the logistics of the project.

4. How do we train teachers to integrate the arts into the curriculum?

WPCA has selected a talented and well versed paper maker to participate in this project. She has vast experience with teachers in rural, urban, private and public schools. One of her main goals in any residency is to show teachers in all subject areas that students can often understand the material easier and relate it to their everyday lives by using the arts to illustrate this relationship.

Our Education Coordinator also tries to integrate and relate the art projects that the children create to their everyday world so that they see that the arts affect them in many aspects from the design or their furniture, their clothing, the colors of road sound barriers or billboard posts.

5. How will the students get to WPCA for the paper making.

The students will walk the four blocks from Kagel School to WPCA for the paper making sessions. They will be escorted by their teachers, teacher aids and parents.

6. How will you and the school assess the impact of the residency on the student's overall learning?

The teachers and staff will be asked to evaluate the student's enthusiasm for the project and the related classroom work. Parents will be asked about the feedback the children had at home with their family and friends. Because students will have to keep up with all their regular work in addition to the paper making project activities, teachers will be asked if the students readily did their extra homework and regular assignments to ensure their participation in the project.